Praise

Jim Akers has come up with a very helpful new term that can help all of us through difficult times and doubt: Godfidence. And the beauty is that the word speaks for itself. It is a lesson and a reminder all at the same time. God is powerful, loving, present every moment, and best of all he hears us and will always guide us in the right direction. This is a book full of wisdom and joy. It is propelled by captivating stories, Scripture, and honest personal narrative. A perfect book to read with a group from your church for maximum encouragement. I highly recommend it.

—Craig J. Hazen, Ph.D.
Founder and Director, Graduate program in Christian Apologetics, Biola University, Bestselling author, *Five Sacred Crossings* and *Fearless Prayer*

Jim Akers has done something remarkable. He has taken the gospel and put it into a form we can all apply to our everyday lives. We all want to live our lives with meaning, and for many of us, with the intention that we can somehow bless others. In *Godfidence*, Jim shares stories of faith that we can all use to lift us out of our daily grind, rise above our circumstances, and allow us to move forward in strength and confidence—HIS confidence.

—Scott Hamilton, Husband, Father, & Cancer Survivor
NY Times Best Selling Author
Olympic Gold Medalist, Four-time World and U. S. Figure Skating Champion

Godfidence is one of those books you can't read and then ignore. Every believer and small group leader needs to get this book. It is a game-changer!

—Mary Valloni, Author and Co-Founder of Fully Funded Academy

"Despite good intentions and righteous-sounding platitudes, we "card-carrying" Christians are stumbling badly as witnesses of the very one we claim to follow, Jesus Christ. In a deeply personal and engaging style, author Jim Akers pinpoints how the ruse of self-confidence, which has evolved into rampant idolatry, is the major culprit in our spiritual ineptitude. *Godfidence* is a must-read for all of us who depend a little too much on ourselves.
—Harold L. Arnold, Jr., PhD, Author,
Unfair Advantage: A grace-inspired path to winning at marriage

God created us for a great purpose. It's easy to lose sight of our birthright to a divine purpose when life confronts us with challenges and obstacles that shake our self-confidence. In *Godfidence*, Jim Akers exposes the "con" of self-confidence and why it forever keeps you from stepping boldly into your best future. If you want to live a life of impact and do what few people do—finish strong—*Godfidence is* a must-read.
—Akbar Gbajabiamila, Host of *American Ninja Warrior* and of *The Talk*. Author of *Everyone Can Be a Ninja*

Powerful! After Jim's #1 New Release—*Tape Breakers*, I've been hoping he'd write another. *Godfidence*, and it's companion study guide, uniquely teaches you how to gain confidence that is lasting and unshakable.
—Niccie Kliegl, Founder, Fulfill Your Legacy and Talk Show Host for Living Within the Sweet Spot.

Godfidence is more than simply a new way of thinking. It's a transformative way of living that will leave a lasting impact on you. It's your guide to discovering who God created you to be and how He wants to give you the victorious life you have been searching for! Confidence is not enough. What you need is Godfidence.
—Rich Green, Campus Pastor
Compass Christian Church
Colleyville, TX

In a society so focused on 'I,' Akers gives the reader practical guidance on how to fight the cultural current of misplaced confidence by taking it off of ourselves and onto God. This practical life reorientation fuels a humility that generates the power to transform those we love and lead. If you are looking for ways to cultivate a life of humility 'Godfidence' is a good first step.
—Samuel Parsons, DMIN - Pastor, Preacher, Teacher, and Friend

What's the source of your confidence? Jim Akers takes you on a journey where you learn to be confident in a way never before imagined possible. Jim has discovered the source. The source who never forsakes. *Godfidence* maps a strategy I wished I had learned much earlier.
—Aaron Walker, Founder, View From The Top and Author of View From the Top: Living a Life of Significance

Jim Akers speaks from experience. He knows what it's like to have what appears sure and certain wiped out in the blink of an eye. But he knows there's something far greater than self-made confidence—the supreme value of gaining unshakable Godfidence—a new level relationship with God where you know it is well with your soul no matter what happens.
—Joan L. Turley, CEO and Founder, Salon and Spa Made Simple, Author, *Sacred Work in Secular Places*

Confidence is a powerful word to understand, to study and live out smartly. Jim's book is a powerful must read if you want to advance your thinking, perspectives and the right results. *Godfidence* has me thinking and I love thinking.
—Tony Jeary, The RESULTS Guy™, Author, *Strategic Parenting*, *Advice Matters*, and *Results Matter*

It takes "Godfidence" to orchestrate a move amid a pandemic and government shutdown, but that's exactly what Jim Akers did as he wrote this book. *Godfidence* is a raw, transparent expose of human confidence when shaken by circumstances. Jim's poignant storytelling, vulnerability, and wisdom come together to create a must-read book that will transform how you live!

—Ed Norwood, husband, father, and author of *Be A Giant Killer: Overcoming Your Everyday Goliaths*

Jim Akers is a voice of impact in a time when we need powerful leaders. The message of *Godfidence* comes at a time when our world needs clarity, credibility, and courage. Akers brings all three together and provides a tool to give us the advantage of hope in an out of control world.

—Tony Colson, Pastor and Award-Winning Author, *Your Divine DNA*

"What did Abraham, Moses, Ruth, David, Esther, Mary, Peter, and most of our cherished biblical heroes have in common – they were all unqualified for the task that God had called them to. But they had something else in common that was crucial – they all surrendered their lives to God and trusted that He would deliver the outcome in spite of their shortcomings. In other words, they had 'Godfidence'. This book reveals one of the most important truths for every follower of Christ to understand: what God intends to do through you involves you but does not depend on you. He doesn't need your ability, but he does require your availability—unconditionally. Give him that, and then just watch what he does."

—Richard Stearns, President Emeritus of World Vision US, author of *The Hole in Our Gospel* and *Lead Like it Matters to God*

GODFIDENCE

Reliable Confidence for Navigating
an Unreliable World

JIM AKERS

Copyright © 2021 Jim Akers
All rights reserved.

No part of this publication may be reproduced, stored in a retrieval system, or transmitted in any for or my any means—for example, electronic, photocopy, recording—without the prior written permission. The only exception is brief quotations in printed reviews.

Unless otherwise indicated, Scripture quotations are from the Holy Bible, New International Version®. NIV®. Copyright © 1973, 1978, 1984, 2011 by Biblica, Inc.™ Used by permission of Zondervan. All rights reserved worldwide. www.zondervan.com. The "NIV" and "New International Version" are trademarks registered in the United States Patent and Trademark Office by Biblica, Inc.™

Amplified Bible—Scripture quotations marked "AMP" are taken from the Amplified® Bible, Copyright © 1954, 1958, 1962, 1964, 1965, 1987 by The Lockman Foundation. Used by permission. www.Lockman.org

(ESV) – The Holy Bible: English Standard Version—Scripture quotations marked "ESV" are from the ESV Bible® (The Holy Bible, English Standard Version®), copyright © 2001 by Crossway Bibles, a publishing ministry of Good News Publishers. Used by permission. All rights reserved.
http://www.crossway.org

The Message—Scripture quotations marked "MSG" or "The Message" are taken from The Message. Copyright 1993, 1994, 1995, 1996, 2000, 2001, 2002. Used by permission of NavPress Publishing Group.
http://www.navpress.com/

Song Title: Somewhere In The Middle Song ID: 1156883 Song Writers: John Mark Hall, Be Essential Songs (BMI) / My Refuge Music (BMI) / (admin at EssentialMusicPublishing.com. All rights reserved. Used by permission.
License #: 15760210224143611

ISBN Paperback: 978-1-64746-953-5
ISBN Hardback: 979-8-9855609-0-9
ISBN Ebook: 978-1-64746-955-9

Library of Congress Control Number: 2021922613

Author Academy Elite, Powell, OH

The Internet addresses, phone numbers, or company or product information in this book are accurate at the time of publication. They are provided as a resource. Jim Akers or the publisher do not endorse them or vouch for their content or permanence.

CONTENTS

Foreword xi
Introduction xv

PART ONE
YOU ONLY FINISH ONCE

Chapter 1: The Con of Self-Confidence 5
Chapter 2: The Power of Godfidence 10

PART TWO
GETTING LOST IN CONFIDENCE

Chapter 3: The Myth of Self Reliance 21
Chapter 4: The Myth of Positive Thinking 26
Chapter 5: The Myth of Experience 33
Chapter 6: The Myth of False Identity 38

Chapter 7:	The Myth of Mediocrity	42
Chapter 8:	The Wilderness Mentality	47
Chapter 9:	Timeless Means Timeless	52
Chapter 10:	Bad Things Do Happen to Good People	58
Chapter 11:	Hey, You're Drifting	64
Chapter 12:	Blurry Vision—Spiritual Blindness	70

PART THREE

THE SOLUTION
FIVE BUILDING BLOCKS FOR BUILDING THE RELIABLE CONFIDENCE YOU NEED FOR FINISHING STRONG

Chapter 13:	The Process Recalculating—Fix Your Eyes On Jesus	80
Chapter 14:	The Invitation What Do We Do With Jesus' Invitation?	87
Chapter 15:	Uncovering Your Purpose Our Identity in Christ—Purposeful and Powerful	93
Chapter 16:	Claiming God's Promises A Promise is a Promise—Leaning on the Promise Maker	99
Chapter 17:	Dress the Part Putting on the Full Armor of God	105

PART FOUR

INTRODUCTION
LIVING IN DAILY GODFIDENCE

Chapter 18:	Truth, Faith, Prayer—Holy Anticipation and Expectation	118

Chapter 19: Take Every Thought Captive	125
Chapter 20: Put First Things First	134
Chapter 21: Build A Deepwater Faith	139
Chapter 22: Keep Your Eye on the Finish Line	147

PART FIVE
FINISHING STRONG

Chapter 23: Make Room for God to Surprise You	157
Chapter 24: One-On-One with Jesus	164
Acknowledgments	171
Appendix	175
Endnotes	177

FOREWORD

Based on first impressions, I can usually spot someone with self-confidence. They carry themselves with a certain sense of poise and presence. They look you in the eye, speak with a relaxed eloquence, and demonstrate that they're comfortable in their own skin. They inspire you to believe in their capabilities and to trust in their judgment. Doubts and fears seem remote and unthinkable because they project the kind of strength that can handle whatever life throws their way. They appear to have something that draws others to them.

As a pastor, teacher, and leader for more than three decades, I've encountered hundreds if not thousands of people who exuded this kind of unshakable confidence when I met them. Once we became better acquainted, however, I've also seen the majority of these individuals peel away the veneer of their confidence to reveal their deep struggles, ongoing frustrations, and bitter disappointments. I've learned that sometimes the people who seem the most secure are the ones who struggle the most.

Christians are certainly not immune to this struggle. I especially have a heart for pastoring my fellow pastors, and many of them experience the tension of being confident before their congregations while feeling deeply insecure inside. They want to serve but often wrestle with having the strong, bedrock confidence to do what God calls them to do—which frequently requires them to step out of their comfort zones and stretch their resources.

I can more than relate to this push-pull because I still get nervous sometimes and have doubts about my own ability to serve, to preach, and to lead. So I share with them what stabilizes and relaxes me when I'm stressed about something I've never done before or face unfamiliar challenges: remembering that it's not up to me. Simply put, it's summed up by what my friend Jim Akers calls "Godfidence."

Jim knows firsthand the difference between confidence based on personal experiences, talents, and achievements and confidence based on a relationship with the Lord. As a high-powered executive in an elite Fortune 50 company, Jim thrived on working hard to exceed goals, strengthen teams, and increase profits. When this role and its privileges disappeared overnight, Jim faced the true basis for his identity and security at a new and deeper level. He realized just how much he had relied on his own abilities to make life work the way he wanted it to work. He saw how he focused on pleasing others and winning their favor. With his limitations suddenly exposed, Jim realized the only source for rebuilding his life was to make God the divine architect.

Persevering through his pain, anger, and confusion, Jim discovered how to live in the confidence that only comes from relying on the Lord in all areas of life, the basis for this unique and distinct term. "Godfidence is living in the full assurance of the hope we have in Jesus," Jim explains, "and giving ourselves daily to His invincible purpose. What makes this incredible is that it's not about adding something you don't have. Godfidence is about plugging into something you already possess."

Drawing on the wisdom that only comes from enduring trials, studying God's Word, and drawing closer to Him, Jim has created a field guide for anyone who wants to trust God for more rather than settle for what they can do themselves. *Godfidence* is a resource that I wish someone would have handed to me early in my ministry, but I'm nonetheless thrilled now to learn from Jim and to pass along his book to so many of the people I pastor and mentor.

Whether you feel self-confident based on your own abilities, or you've been humbled by circumstances exposing your human limitations, *Godfidence* directs you to the only source of lasting peace, infinite power, and eternal security—the grace of God, the love of Jesus, and the power of the Holy Spirit.

—Chris Hodges
Pastor, Church of the Highlands
Author of *What's Next?* and *Out of the Cave*

INTRODUCTION

I wrote this book because I was desperate to regain my lost confidence. Before sharing what I've learned about claiming God's blessing of lasting and unshakeable confidence—Godfidence—let me provide some context by asking you a question. What's your first thought when you think about confidence? You likely didn't land on one idea. Confidence is not that simple. It is a seemingly fleeting force that continually shapes and influences our lives.

> **What's your first thought when you think about confidence?**

We dream of what we can achieve by conjuring up more self-confidence and lament what might have been if we possessed greater faith in ourselves. You've surely felt its strength in moments of victory. But I am equally sure that you've been disappointed by its absence when you needed it most.

Wouldn't our lives be much easier if we could tap into confidence on demand? Our smartphone would be so much smarter if it could connect us to self-confidence. We covet self-confidence. It is empowering—seemingly magical. Unshakeable inner belief sparks a sense of invincibility that enables us to do our best when it matters most.

There is an essential and frustrating quality of self-confidence. On the one hand, we need it for life as much as the air we breathe. On the other hand, unlike the air we breathe, we can't reliably draw in self-confidence when we need it the most—or can we? When I pose the question, people seem equally perplexed by this dilemma. Ask them about times they felt most self-confident in their lives, and you quickly realize self-confidence is elusive.

The Rise Before the Fall

I grew up in a lower-middle-class home, raised and supported by loving parents who grew up poor—very poor. They instilled the value and importance of faith, grace, hard work, and doing your best in my sister, brother, and me. I translated "doing my best" into "being the best." I framed everything as a competition and placed more importance on winning than on exploring faith and accepting the gift of grace.

While I didn't win at everything, I grew fiercely competitive, as was demonstrated by an attitude that could only be described as cocky and arrogant. This mentality fostered an externally bold self-confidence that helped me compensate for weaknesses and quiet my fears. Over time, I developed the belief that I'd always be able to breathe in confidence. And even if I wasn't entirely confident, I'd fake it until my deficient self-belief caught up.

Now You Have It — Now You Don't

I believed self-confidence was the key to achievement. With enough confidence, you could achieve anything you set your mind to. I studied and nurtured self-confidence, intending to win at whatever I deemed to be important. My process was simple—dream up great plans, set big goals, and get to work.

After I had worked it all out, I might even pray for God to bless my pursuits.

When I graduated with honors from Washington State University and was named Outstanding Senior in Marketing, I was on my way. My career got off to a fast start with Owens-Corning Fiberglas (OCF) when I was named Top New Sales Professional. The next year, I became the youngest winner of OCF's prestigious Sales Builder Award. OCF rewarded my performance with two promotions and paid for my MBA. This succession of achievements validated my belief that I was on the road to success and further fueled my self-confidence.

Now just a couple years removed from college, I had it all figured out. So, I decided to write and publish my first book—"How to Win the Achievement Game." It helped open the door to being named Vice President of Sales for a $500MM distribution company at the age of 29. The company's success made it a prime target for acquisition. When International Paper acquired us, it opened more doors for advancement. I received several promotions and eventually became one of the youngest Group Vice Presidents in IP's 100-year history.

I got good at winning—awards, promotions, titles, income, houses, club memberships, and cars. Translating my victories into proof of God's approval and endorsement, I'd dream up new plans, set new goals, ask God for His blessing, and get to work. I experienced periodic setbacks and disappointments, but my deep reserve of self-confidence didn't allow them to deter me. I always found a way to breathe self-confidence back in until March 3, 2013.

At this point, my self-confident-fueled ascension had spanned approximately 28,252,800 minutes. But in a blind-siding meeting that took less than 45 minutes, .000162% of my time on this planet, my self-confidence was blown away. Just weeks after successfully leading a major strategic initiative that required me to travel between Southern California and Cincinnati 50 times while maintaining my primary responsibility of running a nearly $1B business, I was told my career with the organization was finished. I'll tell you more about this story later.

I intellectually understood that losing a career was a big deal. But it turned out to be more traumatic than I ever imagined. It's embarrassing to admit the depth of my ignorance, lack of empathy, and willingness to insulate myself from the experiences of people who lost their confidence. Anyone who has confronted divorce, illness, loss of a loved one, failed exams, business losses, performance failures, broken relationships, or the changes that come with aging knows the struggle.

I struggled mightily. The self-confidence that had readily elevated my performance vanished. Everything I thought about doing felt monumentally more difficult—even impossible. What happened? I started to wonder, what would it take to rekindle my self-confidence? I felt a growing sense of urgency to reclaim my confidence—understand how it worked, how I lost it, where to find it, and how to make sure I didn't lose it again.

If you were observing me, I might not have appeared to look desperate—assuredly not defeated. But on the inside, it was different. For the first time in my life, I felt truly lost. If I hadn't understood why the graveholes of alcohol, drugs, and infidelity were magnets for lost and searching souls, I did now. There were times my anger, resentment, and bitterness consumed my thoughts. Their weight kept pushing me toward peeking into these graves. I was one slippery step away from falling in. The knock of depression on the door of my heart and mind grew persistently louder.

> **Under pressure, we naturally rely on what is most familiar and comfortable to us. It's where we feel most at home—reliantly self-confident.**

Under pressure, we naturally rely on what is most familiar and comfortable to us. It's where we feel most at home—reliantly self-confident. Standing in this unfamiliar territory, I grew desperate for help. Home base, for me, was taking charge and dreaming up a new plan. My self-reliant determination, while admirable in the eyes of many, exhausted me. Eventually, I gave up. Quit. Now I understood what it meant to come to the end of myself. Now I was ready to take my first step on the road to understanding the source of reliable confidence.

A Change of Plans

When your plans fall apart, it is disorienting. If you crash hard enough, it feels defeating. I saw myself victoriously running through the finish line—hearing God say, "Well done." But now I had no vision. I couldn't see the finish line. The stark reality was my vision didn't extend much beyond the end of the day. C. S. Lewis captures the emotion perfectly, writing, "We can ignore even pleasure. But pain insists upon being attended to. God whispers to us in our pleasures, speaks in our conscience, but shouts in our pains: it is His megaphone to rouse a deaf world."[1]

News flash! God will disrupt our circumstances until He gets our attention. It's a fact. Just look back at the lives of Abraham, Moses, Ruth, David, Jonah, Mary, and Paul. Disruptions are not reserved solely for Biblical personalities. God uses disruptions to point us back to him. Look into the the journeys of Louis Zamperini (we'll look at Louis' life later); Chuck Colson, Special Counsel to President Richard Nixon;[2] country music icon, Dolly Parton;[3] Phil Robertson of "Duck Dynasty" fame;[4] Kathie Lee Gifford,[5] co-host of "Live!" with Regis Philbin; Tim Allen, star of "Home Improvement;"[6] "Fixer Upper" star, Joanna Gaines;[7] musician, Jeremy Camp;[8] Hall of Fame basketball legend, "Pistol Pete" Maravich[9]; or U2 lead singer, Bono[10] to name just a few.

God wants our attention! Now he had mine. When I accepted that God was in the midst of my circumstances, I began to see Him with fresh eyes—not too clearly at first, due to self-inflicted myopia. But with time and effort, He came into view. I received the gift of spiritual Lasik eye surgery one morning while reading Jeremiah 29:11, NIV.

> When I accepted that God was in the midst of my circumstances, I began to see Him with fresh eyes—not too clearly at first, due to self-inflicted myopia.

> "For I know the plans I have for you," declares the Lord, "plans to prosper you and not to harm you, plans to give you hope and a future."

You likely recognize this passage as an often-used verse of inspiration and encouragement. It popularly appears on coffee cups, posters, greeting cards, and t-shirts. If you are looking for confidence, what more do you need to know than the "Lord plans to prosper you…to give you hope and a future"? It feels so sufficient and satisfying. Why read any further—right?

May I have your attention, please?

Because verse eleven was the only passage highlighted on page 845 in my nearly 40-year-old Bible, there was no firm proof I had ever read any further. But this time, I kept reading.

> "'Then you will call on me and come and pray to
> me, and I will listen to you. You will seek me and
> find me when you seek me with all your heart.
> I will be found by you,' declares the Lord."
> —Jeremiah 29:12-14, NIV

As I kept reading over these verses, I realized the promise in verse eleven is conditional. It is what follows "the Lord declaring his plans for you and me" that activates God's declared promise. It was up to me to pray and seek God with my whole heart. Then I would harvest His promise of plans to give me hope and a future.

> Looking for confidence outside of that which is instilled and ordained by God is a "con."

This was the first step in my new plan—seek God first. When I started seeking Him first and praying earnestly, my vision improved. He helped me see and understand the problem with self-confidence. Here it is—looking for confidence outside of that which is instilled and ordained by God is a "con."

Pressure Cooked

A. W. Tozer said, "The only book that should ever be written is one that flows up from the heart, forced out by the inward pressure."[11] The pressure to write this book was pressed up by desire and pain. The desire to finish well—"to press on toward the goal to win the prize for which God has called me heavenward in Christ Jesus" (Philippians 3:14) and the pain of discovering confidence secured outside of that which we find in Jesus is a "con" that assures our failure.

The Answer is God-confidence — Godfidence

What would it feel like to be welcomed into heaven and hear, "Well done, good and faithful servant" (Matthew 25:21, ESV)? Picture it. I can only imagine what a glorious scene this will be. Can you picture it in your mind's eye?

My heart skips a beat thinking, even for a second, about being conned into losing this eternal prize. Godfidence is essential for finishing well—to know Christ, make Him known, bring glory to God in all we do, and enjoy Him forever. I am using Godfidence to describe living in the full assurance of the hope we have in Jesus and giving ourselves over to His invincible purpose.

The Journey to Godfidence

As you embark on this journey to Godfidence with me, there are a few more things you should know. This book was not easy to write for a lot of reasons. As hard as it is to admit, I am stubborn and prideful. Thus this writing journey required me to lose myself, which I fought and continue to fight. As a result, I regularly found myself staring at a blank computer screen stuck in between assured belief this book was needed and persistent fear that I had no business writing this book.

I am writing this book from the perspective of my Christian faith and how I've come to understand living out the joy I have in Christ—to finish well. Thus, I recognize self-reliance comes naturally. But within each of us is a hole that nothing but Christ can fill up. Charles Colson sums it up beautifully, writing, "All human beings yearn, deep in their hearts, for deliverance from sin and guilt.

Many try to suppress the longing, to rationalize it away, to mute it with lesser answers. But ultimately, it is impossible to evade."[12]

I tried to evade Jesus for a long time by treating him as an accessory—nice to have alongside, but not relinquishing control. Godfidence is about the journey to making Him my world. What spills out in these pages is God's hand at work in my life. I desperately want to finish well, finish strong, and help you do the same.

I've divided our journey to Godfidence together into five parts.

- Part One: You Only Finish Once
- Part Two: The Problem with Confidence
    - Looking for confidence in all the wrong places
    - Losing confidence for all the wrong reasons
- Part Three: Godfidence—Plugging into Reliable Confidence
- Part Four: Living in Daily Godfidence—Strategies for Finishing Well
- Part Five: The Finish Line

Be sure; finishing is hard. History shows that for many (too many), we die with the dreams God placed on our hearts unattended. Godfidence is about finishing life well—to glorify God and enjoy Him forever by running persistently in God's strength, guidance, and power. If you want to finish well, finish strong, you are in the right place.

> Godfidence is about finishing life well—to glorify God and enjoy Him forever by running persistently in God's strength, guidance, and power.

Thank you for joining me on this journey to Godfidence. When we step into God-confidence—Godfidence—we invite God to do a mighty work within us so He can do an even mightier work through us.

PART ONE
YOU ONLY FINISH ONCE

"Begin with the end in mind."
—Stephen Covey

In recent years, acronyms popularized by social media have become part of our cultural lexicon. They are "hip." If you have to ask what they mean, you might find yourself looking up "OKB," which is short for "OK Boomer." It's not a badge of honor or a sign of respect—you've just been told you're out of touch. It's not an age problem. It's a thinking problem.

Many of these acronyms were once found exclusively on social media. Today, we use them as texting shorthand. They are part of our everyday conversations. A few stand out:

- FOMO: fear of missing out
- FOPO: fear of other people's opinions
- YOLO: you only live once

Do we fear missing out? Only if we are breathing. We all have scars from missing out on something in our past. Do we fear other people's opinions? Who hasn't stopped short of taking action because we feared what other people would say—even people whose opinions shouldn't have been a deciding factor?

The Truth About The Finish Line

Will you only live once? Unequivocally yes—we all dream of finishing strong. But that's not the way the story is going to end. I think it ultimately sorts out like this—everyone starts, few will finish, and rare are those who triumphantly cross the finish line. This brings us to the simple answer to why confidence matters—you only finish once—YOFO! If you are going to fulfill your greatest purpose and highest calling, confidence is required.

> On the road to the finish line, there is a high probability you'll stumble and fail despite the fact God embeds the desire to finish well deep within each of our souls.

Looking back through history confirms finishing life strong is a daunting challenge—a rare but not impossible accomplishment. On the road to the finish line, there is a high probability you'll stumble and fail despite the fact God embeds the desire to finish well deep within each of our souls.

A Surprising Failure To Finish

The Fuller Theological Seminary took a close look at the 2930 people mentioned by name in the Bible. Upon close examination, there was adequate data on 100 of these people to evaluate how well they finished in life. Ultimately they found that only one-third ended well. They all started strong. The majority who failed fell in the second half of their lives.

How could this happen? It's not as if they didn't know what to do. Everyone who stumbled knew what was required to be successful. Each of them possessed a deep and abiding knowledge of God. They clearly understood their mission. God equipped them with the proper tools. But they failed to apply what they knew to how they lived their lives.[13] They got disconnected from God's protection and power.

History is both a powerful and unforgiving teacher. Wisdom for the ages tells us, "Those who cannot remember the past are condemned to repeat it."[14] We kick ourselves when we make avoidable mistakes, lamenting, "I knew better," or "When am I ever going to learn!" Our lives are a collection of experiences—experience is inevitable. However, learning from our experience and applying the lessons of history are optional.

> **History is both a powerful and unforgiving teacher.**

Learning from our experiences and history should be enough to keep us from stumbling on our way to the finish line. But knowledge is not enough. Somewhere along the path of our journey, we lose sight of the goal—you only finish once (YOFO). Paul provided keen insight into our dilemma, writing,

> "I do not consider myself yet to have taken hold of it. But one thing I do: Forgetting what is behind and straining toward what is ahead, I press on toward the goal to win the prize for which God has called me heavenward in Christ Jesus."
> —Philippians 3:13b-14, NIV

The ultimate goal for your life is to finish strong. I am defining finishing strong to mean knowing Christ and making Him known. It's the pursuit of bringing God glory, fulfilling our assignments, and enjoying Him forever. Because YOFO—you only finish once—it is essential to understand that "God did not send you to enter the Christian life but to finish it. Not to quit, but to recommit. Not to start it, but to end it."[15] To finish strong!

> **"God did not send you to enter the Christian life but to finish it. Not to quit, but to recommit. Not to start it, but to end it."**

The journey to finishing strong begins with understanding why self-confidence is a con and discovering the power of Godfidence.

CHAPTER 1
THE CON OF SELF-CONFIDENCE

> "If you have built castles in the air, your work
> need not be lost; that is where they should be.
> Now put the foundations under them."
> —Henry David Thoreau

Living your best life and finishing strong is all about self-confidence! A multi-million dollar industry thrives on getting us to believe that everything in life would be better if we only had more self-confidence—just listen to the self-help gurus.

The seeds for this industry can be traced back at least 100 years to William James—the father of modern psychology. James said, "The reason so many people never fulfill their potential is not because of a lack of intelligence, opportunity, or resources, but because of a lack of belief, or faith, in themselves."

Could achieving success and finishing well in life be any easier? All we need to do is dial up our self-confidence and we've got it—look inside of yourself until you find it.

More Confidence, Please!

What would you do with more self-confidence—secure a better job, ask for a raise, take more risks, ignore the opinions of others, be more decisive, accept feedback more readily, be happier, or be healthier? These are the questions the self-help gurus ask to help you uncover your hidden confidence. It's exciting to think of the possibilities.

An article in *Psychology Today* opens, "Self-confidence is linked to almost every element involved in a happy and fulfilling life...Understanding the benefits of [self-confidence] is an important first step toward living your best life." Researchers say your best life includes less fear and anxiety, greater motivation and resilience, improved relationships, willingness to accept your weaknesses and failings, and a stronger sense of your authentic self.[16]

Well, okay then! It is simple. Sign me up. "I'll have an order of the 'best life' please and throw in a side of vacation. Oh, and if it's not too much trouble, bring me a slice of financial freedom for dessert."

What is Self-Confidence?

The bible of self-confidence is pop culture. Just repeat after me, "Trust yourself;" "Promote yourself;" "Cast a positive light on everything you are doing;" "Be true to yourself because you are the one that counts;" "Fake it until you make it;" "Fake it even if you are not making it;" "Don't let anyone know you are struggling'" and "Play nice as long as it helps you win." Pixar and Disney preach the gospel of self-confidence. They wrap these messages up in cute animated movies we accept as an accurate view of reality and what we, too, should value. We don't question these messages. Who argues with or questions a

> The philosophy of self-confidence is, "I am going to take my cues from the world of pop culture about how I define success and what I value."

cute animated character anyway? Instead, we use these messages to inspire self-reliant confidence.

The philosophy of self-confidence is, "I am going to take my cues from the world of pop culture about how I define success and what I value." This worldview defines today's "American Dream." Ambition fueled by the pursuit of life, liberty, and happiness—"Success on my terms."

Self-confidence relies on wealth, power, and prestige to measure success. It's the existentialist's scoreboard. The underlying philosophy is, "What I do determines who I am and the success I achieve—I set the goal, I determine the outcome, and I define what's valuable." This thinking, dating back to the 16th century, ultimately separated us from God. Apart from God, we lost our sense of absolute truth. The problem with being separated from God's truth is that we become spiritually ill and get lured into the trap of self-confidence—the false belief that the key to happiness and prosperity lies within us.

Apart from God, we lost our sense of absolute truth.

The Problem with Self-Confidence

Be sure of this: Self-confidence is incapable of producing peace or lasting joy. Regardless of where we start from in life, self-confidence ultimately brings us face-to-face with our limitations. We either fall short (fail) and realize that our life will not turn out as we envisioned. Or, we achieve our loftiest goals and dreams only to realize it wasn't worth the price we paid. In a moment of lucid reality, we can't believe the foundation of self-confidence we bet our life on is crumbling beneath our feet. Either way, we lose it all.

Regardless of where we start from in life, self-confidence ultimately brings us face-to-face with our limitations.

The Con of Self-Confidence

I am not arguing that confidence is not essential—it is. Confidence is incredibly valuable. But you won't find the reliable confidence you need to finish strong by looking within yourself. Paul tells us it's a con, writing,

> "For no one can lay a foundation other than that which is laid, which is Jesus Christ."
> —1 Corinthians 3:11

Satan is the master *con* artist. Jesus addressing the Pharisees warns us, saying,

> "Why do you not understand what I say? It is because you cannot bear to hear my word. You are of your father the devil, and your will is to do your father's desires. He was a murderer from the beginning, and does not stand in the truth, because there is no truth in him. When he lies, he speaks out of his own character, for he is a liar and the father of lies."
> —John 8:43-44, ESV

Satan—the master *con* artist, the purveyor of deception, and the author of lies—orchestrates the *con*. He purposefully leads us towards worldly self-confidence—*con*fidence. He relishes in getting us to look for confidence in all the wrong places. He celebrates when he leads us to lose our confidence for all the wrong reasons. It's the nature of his character. His intention is clear—distract us, cloud our calling, and steal the glorious and victorious finish God has planned for us.

Place Your Bet

Are you a gambler? Willing to bet your life on the belief that self-confidence is not a con? I didn't think I was a gambler until I honestly contemplated the role self-confidence played in my life. Gambling, by definition, is "taking a risk in the hope of a favorable outcome." It's hard for me to admit that I bet on myself. I bought into the *con*. Yes, I believed I could finish well by being reliantly self-confident. Surprise, most of us do.

Go ahead, roll the dice, spin the wheel, and hope you finish strong. You are free to choose—we all are. We like to remind the world we are free to choose. But from both experience and observation, I can confirm that choosing is not free. Every choice comes at a price—including responsibility and consequences that commonly don't present themselves immediately. The price of self-confidence is pride. "Pride comes before disaster, and arrogance before a fall" (Proverbs 16:18, CEB).

> Every choice comes at a price—including responsibility and consequences that commonly don't present themselves immediately.

Peter's Self-Confidence

Peter said he'd never deny Jesus. He boldly proclaimed he'd go to prison—even die first. Even after Jesus tells Peter he will deny Him three times, Peter scoffs at the suggestion. His reply shouts of self-confidence. "Lord, you don't know how strong, tough, and courageous I am. I won't fail. Nothing could make me deny you." In his self-confidence, Peter tells Jesus he is wrong. Note to self: this is a bad idea.

> "Then he began to invoke a curse on himself and to swear, 'I do not know the man.' And immediately the rooster crowed. And Peter remembered the saying of Jesus, 'Before the rooster crows, you will deny me three times.' And he went out and wept bitterly."
> —Matthew 26:74-75, ESV

You only finish once (YOFO). Do you want to finish strong? Choosing self-confidence—*con*fidence—is a losing bet. *Con*fidence guarantees we'll stumble on our way to the finish line.

CHAPTER 2
THE POWER OF GODFIDENCE

"He has made everything beautiful in its time. He has also set eternity in the human heart; yet no one can fathom what God has done from beginning to end."
—Ecclesiastes 3:11, NIV

It was hard to imagine that the very thing I thought was essential to living a victorious life had failed me. I couldn't help but wonder, "Was I the only one who got *conned*?" I was both relieved and perplexed to discover I was not alone. But it didn't make the *con* easier to accept—pride is stubborn that way. Honestly, who willingly admits to being *conned*—right? We readily resist disclosing we messed up. It's part of our fallen nature. But thankfully, it's God's nature to pursue us. As God helped me see my pride as an obstacle, He helped me see what I missed.

Can we agree that when life confronts us with an unwelcome change, we fear to let go of what we've known? Being told we must take a new path, especially one that is not of our choosing and may include loss—even pain and suffering—is frightening. Not even the most *con*fident amongst us volunteer for these assignments because deep down we know that self-confidence (*con*fidence) is not enough to win the prize and finish strong. It's a losing bet. Deep in our souls, we know something is missing.

You only finish once (YOFO). Pause and think about this for a moment—we get one shot. For the longest time, I wanted to look back. But you and I know there are no do-overs. What lies in our past is done. Can we agree to leave it there for the moment and focus on the one thing we can control at this moment—our next, right, best step? Take a step with me into Godfidence.

> Godfidence—God•confidence —is living in the full assurance of the hope we have in Jesus and giving ourselves daily to His invincible purpose.

Diving Into Godfidence

"A man is never the same after he simultaneously sees his utter despair and Christ's unbending grace."
—Max Lucado

Godfidence— God•confidence —is living in the full assurance of the hope we have in Jesus and giving ourselves daily to His invincible purpose. What makes this incredible is that it's not about adding something you don't have. Godfidence is about plugging into something you already possess.

We access and connect to Godfidence when we accept the gift of God's grace and use it as the framework for how we understand the world and our place in it. The word confidence (or its close derivatives) is used 54 times in the King James Version and 60 times in the New International Version of the Bible. The majority of uses concern trust in people, circumstances, or God.[17] Because Godfidence is grounded in absolute truth—God's living word—it is the only reliable solution to *con*fidence. Steve Farrar, the author of *Finishing Strong*,

> Because Godfidence is grounded in absolute truth—God's living word—it is the only reliable solution to confidence.

describes the umbrella of Godfidence perfectly, writing, "The very gates of hell cannot make us stumble unless we choose to remove ourselves from His protection and power."[18]

Plugging into God's Protection and Power

Trust is born of three dimensions: compassion, character, and competence. Trust rises in proportion to the degree we see these qualities exhibited in the people we follow. We won't follow a leader we don't trust. If they lack compassion, we'll believe they don't care about us. No matter how eloquent they are, we'll see them lacking integrity if we question their character. If they aren't skilled and knowledgeable, we won't see them successfully leading us to the finish line.

> "Trust in the LORD with all your heart, And don't lean on your own understanding. In all your ways acknowledge him, And he will direct your paths."
> —Proverbs 3:5-6, MEV

On what grounds would you choose not to trust God? Would you question his infinite compassion? God wrote the book on compassion—He is love. "Anyone who does not love does not know God, because God is love" (1 John 4:8, NIV). Do you have a problem with His exemplary character? It's incomparable. He is the quintessential purveyor of wisdom, courage, humanity, and justice—transcendent by nature. "Every good gift, every perfect gift, comes from above. These gifts come down from the Father, the creator of the heavenly lights, in whose character there is no change at all" (James 1:17, CEB). Are you going to question God's competence? On what grounds could we possibly challenge His flawless performance? He always delivers perfectly. "I have spoken, and I will bring it to pass; I have purposed, and I will do it" (Isaiah 46:11b, ESV).

Is it That Easy?

In the spirit of full disclosure, I have a love/hate relationship with essential questions because they force me to contemplate my ignorance. We're taught to value answers over questions throughout our lives, which numbs us to the fact that questions are the gateway to spiritual transformation and godly wisdom. Our mind once challenged with a question, never retreats to its previous state. "It is the glory of God to conceal things, but the glory of kings is to search things out" (Proverbs 25:2, ESV). The glory of kings—to finish strong—requires we wrestle with questions.

> We're taught to value answers over questions throughout our lives, which numbs us to the fact that questions are the gateway to spiritual transformation and godly wisdom.

Beyond contemplating the questions about God's compassion, character, and competency, I wondered, "Does God speak to us today?" The process of "searching things out" would be so much easier if I could hear God speak to me. He could friend me on Facebook, send me a text message, or tweet some guidance. While any of these would do, it's not that easy, I think, for a good reason. There is something both powerful and transformational in earnestly searching and seeking.

I labored for years under the pretense that God's silence meant He was inactive. In hindsight, I can see it gave Him time and space to chip away at my pride and open my heart to receive the gift of His grace. I completely underestimated the necessity of seeking God as foundational to receiving His richest blessing. I began to understand that as *con*fidence is extinguished and gives rise to Godfidence, He reveals more to us than we ever imagined.

Silencing Confidence

For most of my life, I read the Bible like a book. I studied it out of obligation. Isn't that what "good Christians" are supposed to do? In effect, approaching God's word like a sterile academic textbook served to silence His voice. When I started reading as if God was speaking to me—directly and personally, the foundations of *con*fidence began to crumble. Deuteronomy 11:22-24 (NIV) is one of the places where I started to see that Godfidence (God-confidence) solved the problem of *con*fidence.

> "If you <u>carefully</u> observe all these commands I am giving you to follow—to love the Lord your God, to walk in <u>all</u> his ways and to <u>hold fast</u> to him—<u>then</u> the Lord will drive out all these nations before you, and you will dispossess nations larger and stronger than you. Every place where you set your foot will be yours."

Focus on four words/phrases: "carefully," "all," "hold fast," and "then." "Carefully" is there to grab our attention. Anytime someone says, "be careful," they're alerting us to clear and present danger. If you have kids or were a kid once (that should cover everyone), you are familiar with the phrase "be careful." So familiar that you likely no longer appropriately connect it to danger. In this text, God is issuing a "Danger Alert"—be careful! He is telling us here that there is a real danger to our well-being if we decide to proceed without Him. He tells us we'll find safety and prosperity in His instructions—rely on them to guide our thinking and actions.

After He says, "carefully observe," He uses the word "all." What does "all" mean? I was speaking at a men's retreat, where I met Pastor Sam Parsons. At one point, Sam asked, "What does 'all' mean?" It cued a loud, perfectly harmonized chorus of voices, "All," they replied. Sam, nodding approval, said, "Exactly! All means all, nothing excluded." Therefore, when God says, "Walk in all His ways," He means ALL His ways—exclude nothing.

When God says, "Walk in all His ways," He means ALL His ways— exclude nothing.

Aware that life is full of noise and distractions, God adds, "Hold fast to [Me]." God is telling them not to lose their focus or worry about the outcome—"keep your eyes on Me." Don't hold on to anyone else or seek any other solution because He will deliver them. Feeling the heat, getting uncomfortable amid the battle? Do not stray; hold fast to Him.

After the instructions, God links His command and encouragement to the outcome with "then." "Then" in this context is a word of condition. Do these things I have told you, "Carefully observe all my commands," "hold fast to me," and "then" I will deliver you.

Think about the significance of this for a moment. The Israelites spent seven years battling thirty-seven nations after they entered the Promised Land. Can you imagine what they might have been thinking? That voice of doubt, discouragement, and frustration starts getting louder. "Wait a minute, Lord, I thought when we arrived in the Promised Land, we would find peace. Ah, can you please tell us why we are fighting to guard and protect the very thing you promised us? How about some peace and quiet, please?"

Lured into *con*fidence, the Israelites took their eyes off the Lord. They misplaced their trust and wasted years wandering around by choosing to rely on their own strength and confidence. The moment they returned their trust to the Lord, they revived their Godfidence and found their way back home.

Thinking About the Finish Line

To finish strong, you must keep your eye on the finish line—YOFO, you only finish once. *Con*fidence is a real obstacle that stands between you and the finish line. The lure of *con*fidence is always looming. In section two, we'll explore how the enemy draws you into the *con* that leads you to look for confidence in all the wrong places and lose confidence for all the wrong reasons.

PART TWO
GETTING LOST IN CONFIDENCE

"As soon as you trust yourself, you will know how to live."
— Johann Wolfgang von Goethe

Self-trust fuels *con*fidence. Willie Sutton, the infamous bank robber, lived by Goethe's proclamation. When Willie was asked why he robbed banks, he replied, "Because that is where the money is." You can't argue with Willie's knowledge or his *con*fidence. Over his 45-year robbery career, he stole over $2,000,000 and escaped prison three times.[19] But "Slick Willie's" logic ignored reality—even the most successful bank robbers eventually end up broke and in jail or dead.

> While our fears, ambitions, and experiences shape the lens through which we see the world, reality can't be swayed by how fervently we believe something to be true. Reality is an unforgiving foe.

The dictionary definition of reality is "The world or the state of things as they actually exist...existence that is absolute, self-sufficient, or objective, and not subject to human decisions or conventions."[20]

While our fears, ambitions, and experiences shape the lens through which we see the world, reality can't be swayed by how fervently we believe something to be true. Reality is an unforgiving foe. It doesn't adjust to accommodate our biases or ignore our erroneous thinking. Thinking about the nature and character of reality presents us with an important question: Why do we look for our confidence in the world? The answer is the same as why Willie Sutton robbed banks. It is where the famous purveyors of worldly success lead us to believe we will find it. The problem with this logic is that it ignores the reality of God's word.

> "Delight yourself in the Lord, and he will give you the desires of your heart. Commit your way to the Lord; trust in him, and he will act."
> —Psalms 37:4-5, ESV

I trusted myself too. Self-trust is opposed to God's instruction. Anything opposed to God is sin, which in its own way is a denial of reality. Not only did I refuse to acknowledge my condition, but I also defended it. J.K. Galbraith beautifully sums up the problem this condition confronts us with, writing, "Faced with a choice between changing one's mind and proving there is no need to do so, almost everyone gets busy with the proof."[21]

I was a walking testimony to Galbraith's observation. It was more comfortable by far to defend my self-made illusion that I was stronger and better off trusting myself than face the reality that my self-trust separated me from God. In researching this book, I didn't find anyone willing to argue otherwise. T. S. Eliot cuts to the heart of the problem, writing,

> "All things become less real, man passes
> From unreality to unreality.
> This man is obstinate, blind, intent
> On self-destruction.
> Passing from deception to deception,

From grandeur to grandeur to final illusion.
Lost in the wonder of his own greatness.
The enemy of society, enemy of himself."²²

Discovering We've Been Conned

Imagine yourself in paradise and being given full dominion over it. Look around; everything you could possibly want is at your disposal. All you need to do is follow one rule. That's it—honor one rule, and it's all yours.

> "You are free to eat from any tree in the garden; but you must not eat from the tree of the knowledge of good and evil, for when you eat from it you will certainly die."
> —Genesis 2:16-17, NIV

Could God's warning be any clearer? It's the first and only warning given to Adam and Eve. He leaves no room for interpretation or confusion, "Eat from this tree and you will die." Should anything more need to be said or done to secure their obedience? What could possibly go wrong—right? Then the "crafty serpent" showed up.

> "You will not certainly die," the serpent said to the woman. "For God knows that when you eat from it your eyes will be opened, and you will be like God, knowing good and evil."
> —Genesis 3:4-5, NIV

God's first and only warning becomes the framework for the first *con* job. A dictionary definition of a *con* job is "an act or instance of duping, swindling, lying, or talking glibly to convince others or get one's way."²³ Be assured the Enemy is a *con* man. The tree he wants you to eat from today is called *con*fidence. He makes self-reliant *con*fidence feel good and smell good. He makes it sparkle, so it catches your eye. He desires to trigger the little voice in your head that

God's first and only warning becomes the framework for the first con job.

says, "With more self-confidence, you can have everything your heart desires." It's all a *con* aimed at getting us to take his bait and destroy our relationship with God and the foundation we need to finish well.

C. S. Lewis said, "We all want progress. But progress means getting nearer to the place where you want to be. And if you have taken a wrong turn, then to go forward does not get you any nearer. If you are on the wrong road, progress means doing an about-turn and walking back to the right road; and in that case, the man who turns back soonest is the most progressive man."[24]

As my research for this book took me more in-depth, I began to see how the *con* started to unfold. It's masterful in its subtlety. You don't see it coming. In search of the missed warning signs, I retraced my steps, looking for the way to get back on the right road Lewis describes. I wish I had understood the reliability of Godfidence before I stumbled so badly. I pray that sharing the lessons I've learned and continue to uncover on my journey to Godfidence will help you avoid my mistakes, encourage you, and provide resources to help you finish well.

In the next ten chapters, we'll dive into signs that warn us we are living in *con*fidence:

- Five myths about *con*fidence—looking for confidence in all the wrong places.

- Five reasons we lose our God-confidence—losing confidence for all the wrong reasons.

"These are all warning markers—DANGER!—in our history books, written down so that we don't repeat their mistakes. Our positions in the story are parallel—they at the beginning, we at the end—and we are just as capable of messing it up as they were. Don't be so naive and self-confident. You're not exempt. You could fall flat on your face as easily as anyone else. Forget about self-confidence; it's useless. Cultivate [Godfidence.]"
—I Corinthians 10:11-12, MSG

CHAPTER 3
THE MYTH OF SELF RELIANCE

"If it is to be, it is up to me."

Just repeat after me, "If it is to be, it is up to me." This is the foundation of self-reliance—I am responsible for my choices and outcomes. I don't need anything outside of myself. Everything I need to learn, grow, and thrive is inside of me—it is up to me. All I need to do is choose confidence and it will be mine. The self-help gurus call these ten simple words the "shortest motivational speech" ever written.

The Myth of Self-Reliance

We are looking for confidence in all the wrong places if we believe we can conjure it up by looking for it within ourselves.

A Poster Boy for Self-Reliance

Louis Zamperini's life was built on these words. As a youth, he broke all the rules, ignored those who tried to direct him, and fought anyone who contested him. He channeled his resilient independence and toughness into running during his teenage years and discovered he possessed an extraordinary talent.

Louis would flirt with becoming the first to run a sub-four-minute-mile and became the youngest distance runner ever to make the U. S. Olympic team. At the 1936 Olympics in Berlin, he ran one of the fastest laps in Olympic history and caught the eye of Adolf Hitler, who shook his hand after the race. Still not one to shy away from what he wanted, Zamperini was nearly shot while attempting to steal a Nazi flag as a souvenir.

Louis enlisted in the Army in 1941 and miraculously skirted death many times while serving as a B-24 bombardier. Shot down over the Pacific Ocean, he spent 47 days drifting at sea. After being captured by the Japanese Navy, he would spend over two hellish years in three different interrogation centers and POW camps. Zamperini, already tough and tested, would survive brutal daily beatings and challenges administered at the hands of the man the prisoners referred to as The Bird (Shizuka Watanabe).

A Public Hero

Zamperini's notoriety after the war increased. He said, "After being declared dead and finding that we'd crashed and survived the 47-day drift and nearly 2,000 miles, you get quite a bit of publicity." Louis' self-reliant attitude, combined with his good looks and remarkable story, made him the perfect "war hero."

In 1946, Louis got married and was traveling the country telling his story. By every outward appearance, Louis was thriving, but on the inside, everything was falling apart. He could not shake the memory of the brutal beatings and emotional hurt inflicted by The Bird. Louis tried to drown the hellish nightmares with alcohol. Falling into the grip of depression, Louis' behavior became unpredictable and violent as he harbored thoughts of how to murder The Bird.

Self-reliance gave him the strength to survive The Bird, but it would not save his family or his life. "I got married, I had a little girl and I continued to drink and continued to party, and my wife refused to go with me," Louis said. "Pretty soon I found myself fading away, to the point where I realized that I was in serious need of help."[25]

Four years after returning from the war, he was still in his Hollywood apartment, drowning in alcohol and making plans to murder The Bird.[26] In October of 1949, Louis' wife, Cynthia, persuaded him into going to hear Billy Graham speak. Louie knew nothing about Billy Graham.

Staying the Course

Louis, operating under the umbrella of "if it is to be, it is up to me," was enraged by Graham's message that self-reliance was a myth. When Graham offered his traditional invitation for salvation, Louis grabbed his wife's arm and stormed out. As he slept that night, The Bird again hijacked Louis' dreams. He awoke feeling the need to return that night to listen to Billy one more time.

Again that night, Graham preached the Gospel as he always did. "God works miracles one after another," he said. "...God says, 'If you suffer, I'll give you the grace to go forward.'" In the grip of suffering the invitation of grace had Louis' attention. But as Graham asked for heads to bow and eyes to close, Louie abruptly stood up and rushed for the street, towing Cynthia behind him. "Nobody's leaving," said Graham. "You can leave while I'm preaching but not now. Everybody is still and quiet. Every head bowed, every eye closed."[27] He asked the faithful to come forward.

Louis's next move was prompted by a recollection Laura Hillenbrand describes perfectly in her biography [*Unbroken*] about Louis' life.

"A memory long beaten back, the memory from which he had run the evening before, was upon him. Louie was on the raft. There was gentle Phil crumpled up before him, Mac's breathing skeleton, endless ocean stretching away in every direction, the sun lying over them, the cunning bodies of the sharks, waiting, waiting, circling. He was a body on a raft, dying of thirst. He felt words whisper from his swollen lips. It was a promise thrown at heaven, a promise he had not kept, a promise he had allowed himself to forget until just this instant: *If you will save me, I will serve you forever.* And then, standing under a circus tent on a clear night in downtown Los Angeles, Louie felt rain falling. It was the last flashback he would ever have. Louie let go of Cynthia and turned toward Graham. He felt supremely alive. He began walking. 'This is it,' said Graham. 'God has spoken to you. You come on.'"[28]

Come Just As You Are

That night when Louis accepted Graham's invitation, he said goodbye to the myth, "If it is to be, it is up to me." This is the moment Louis discarded *con*fidence. Just as he was, Louis walked into the arms of Jesus and embraced Godfidence. He identified it as the first time he felt profound peace—saved by God's divine love. There is more to this story that I'll share later in the book.

> "This is what the Lord says: 'Cursed is the one who trusts in man, who draws strength from mere flesh and whose heart turns away from the Lord. That person will be like a bush in the wastelands; they will not see prosperity when it comes. They will dwell in the parched places of the desert, in a salt land where no one lives.'"
> —Jeremiah 17:5-6, NIV

The enemy's goal is to draw us into the world. Self-help pep-talks like, "If it is to be, it is up to me," encourage us to write a fifth gospel—our own autobiographical gospel, the "gospel according to me." The myth of self-reliance is intoxicating because it elevates our natural desire to be in charge of our life and elevates our importance. Self-reliance is a myth because when we rely solely on our abilities, qualities, and judgment, we will forfeit the protection and guidance required to finish strong. The reality is that when we look for confidence in our own strength, we are heading for disappointment and ultimately defeat.

CHAPTER 4
THE MYTH OF POSITIVE THINKING

*"Our confidence must always be in Christ
and His abilities. Whenever we think we can,
we usually end up failing miserably."*
—A. W. Tozer

My earliest recollection of being coached in the art of positive thinking took place when I was eight years old. After exasperating my third-grade teacher, Mrs. Aikens, with my lack of effort on a project, she exclaimed, "Mr. Akers, can't never did anything. I think you can."

"I think I can" is a mantra of positive thinking. It gained popularity beginning in 1930 when Arnold Munk, under the pen name of Watty Piper, wrote the fairy tale "The Little Engine that Could." In the story, a small engine designed to pull a few cars around the train yard accepts the challenge of pulling a long train of stranded freight cars over the hill, but only after all the big engines declare they are not big enough or powerful enough to do the job. Despite its lack of size and limited power, the little engine succeeds by employing positive thinking. Success is credited to repeating the mantra, "I think I can, I think I can," over and over.

The Myth of Positive Thinking

We are looking for confidence in all the wrong places if we believe that thinking positively and surrounding ourselves with positive affirmations will produce success and happiness. It's all too common to mistake positive thinking with faith grounded in the one true God.

> It's all too common to mistake positive thinking with faith grounded in the one true God.

The Positive Thinking Genie

The myth of positive thinking lures us into the trap of *confidence*. The many popular mantras are alluring. "If you think you can—you can." "Don't worry, be happy." Remind yourself, "Every day in every way, I'm getting better and better." While these affirmations spark the emotions of *con*fidence, they entrap you. You get conned into displacing God with a "positive thinking genie" capable of granting your wishes, making good things happen, and wiping away uncomfortable reality.

I fell into this trap. Reading hundreds of books and listening to thousands of hours of recordings and podcasts on success pumped up my belief that positive thinking would produce reliable confidence. I can take some solace in knowing the lure of "positive thinking" can encircle even the strongest objectors. One such testament is Napoleon Hill's book, *Think and Grow Rich*, selling more than 100 million copies. Hill's best-selling book, published in 1937, is still recognized as one of history's most influential business books.[29]

"I Think I Can" Cures All

"Can you guess what the most successful and happy people think about all day long?" This is a question one of the most sought after motivational speakers and business coaches in the world posted on his Facebook page. "The answer is simple," he said, "Healthy, happy people think about what they want, and how to get it, most of the time. The power of positive thinking and developing a positive attitude are two of the most important qualities a person can have to change their life."[30]

> Anything that derives its strength from self-reliance and sugar-coats reality is going to cause us to stumble.

Self-Deception

How we choose to direct our thinking is critical to finishing strong because our actions are responsive to our thoughts. It shapes the way we process our experiences and make decisions. I've worked hard to train myself to be optimistic. It beats pessimism and laboring under the weight of defeat. But it doesn't change the fact that positive thinking is a *con*. Anything that derives its strength from self-reliance and sugar-coats reality is going to cause us to stumble.

> "He that trusts in his own heart is a fool."
> —Proverbs 28:26, ESV

What if we applied more positive thinking to our past? Would it change our current condition? Could I have restored my career if I contemplated only positive thoughts and blanketed myself in positive affirmations? Positive thinking does not alter reality. It won't defeat a cancer diagnosis, reconcile a broken relationship, change a poor financial decision, cure an addiction, relieve pain, or eliminate suffering. Scars and deep wounds don't heal by putting a bandaid adhered with positive thinking on over them. Positive thinking doesn't change our circumstances. It can only change our perspective on our circumstances.

> Positive thinking doesn't change our circumstances. It can only change our perspective on our circumstances.

A Very Important Lesson

Admiral Jim Stockdale was the highest-ranking United States military officer held as a prisoner of war during the height of the Vietnam War. During his eight-year captivity, he was tortured 20 times. He and his fellow POWs lived with no certainty they would survive, let alone see their families again. After his release, Stockdale became the first three-star officer in the Navy's history to wear both aviator wings and the Congressional Medal of Honor.

In an interview, Admiral Stockdale was asked, "Who didn't make it?" "Oh, that's easy," Stockdale replied, "The optimists. Oh, they were the ones who said, 'We're going to be out by Christmas.' And Christmas would come, and Christmas would go. Then they'd say, 'We're going to be out by Easter.' And Easter would come, and Easter would go. And then Thanksgiving, and then it would be Christmas again. And they died of a broken heart. This is a vital lesson. You must never confuse faith that you will prevail in the end—which you can never afford to lose—with the discipline to confront the most brutal facts of your current reality, whatever they might be."[31]

The Brutal Facts

Positive thinking is a lens into our lives that can keep us from recognizing and dealing effectively with reality. Paul wrote to the Church at Philippi while imprisoned in a Roman jail. He opens with, "Grace to you and peace from God our Father and the Lord Jesus Christ" (Philippians 1:2, ESV). If you read this without considering the brutal facts, you'll miss the light Paul is shining on the myth of positive thinking.

Paul is not kicking back on vacation at the Ritz Carlton. I can't imagine being chained to a Roman soldier is either comfortable or conducive to quiet reflection. He, like Stockdale, understands where he is and the challenges that lie before him. In a moment of beautiful clarity, he uses two foundational words of faith—grace and peace.

"Grace, or karis in Greek, means the unearned, undeserved, unmitigated favor of God. Peace, or shalom in Hebrew, means the unexplainable way God is putting the world back together again amid of all the unsettled chaos still spewing out."[32] We don't access these on our own—grace and peace are gifts God gives us. Paul uses these gifts to tell us where to direct our thinking.

> "Finally, believers, whatever is true, whatever is honorable and worthy of respect, whatever is right and confirmed by God's word, whatever is pure and wholesome, whatever is lovely and brings peace, whatever is admirable and of good repute; if there is any excellence, if there is anything worthy of praise, think continually on these things [center your mind on them, and implant them in your heart]."
> —Philippians 4:8, AMP

Without knowing Paul's condition, you might think that Paul was writing about his optimism—a hope raised on a foundation of positive thinking. But Paul is not claiming any power in his thinking. Just three verses later, he calls out the *con* of positive thinking—resting the strength of his words on the shoulders of Jesus. Paul is not delivering the message, "Embrace the power of positive thinking." He is making it clear that we will find strength sufficient for every circumstance when we embrace Jesus.

> "Not that I am speaking of being in need, for I have learned in whatever situation I am to be content. I know how to be brought low, and I know how to abound. In any and every circumstance, I have learned the secret of facing plenty and hunger, abundance and need. I can do all things through him who strengthens me."
> —Philippians 4:11-13, ESV

Thinking in Strength

There is no "positive thinking genie" you can call on to produce reliable confidence—it's a *con*. Just because you "think you can" doesn't mean you can pull yourself out of a valley. Embracing a "don't worry, be happy" attitude can help prop up your disposition but is powerless to break down any physical or emotional barriers that stand before you. The bottom line is positive thinking doesn't dissolve the scars of disappointment, produce competence in the absence of preparation, or alter reality.

> **There is no "positive thinking genie" you can call on to produce reliable confidence—it's a con.**

Positive thinking didn't work for the disciples either. They didn't want to believe that Jesus would be crucified even though He was training them for his death from the moment He started His ministry.

> "Jesus began to explain to his disciples that he must go to Jerusalem and suffer many things…and that he must be killed and on the third day be raised to life. Peter took him aside and began to rebuke him. 'Never, Lord!' he said. 'This shall never happen to you!'"
> —Matthew 16:21-22, NIV

No amount of positive thinking was going to change Jesus' mission. He never told them, "Hey guys, think positive! Everything is going to be all right. Following me will be easy." Quite the contrary, Jesus emphatically told us, it is not going to be easy. You will face challenges in the world and no amount of positive thinking is going to change it.

> "I have told you these things, so that in me you may have peace. In this world you will have trouble. But take heart! I have overcome the world."
> —John 16:33, NIV

The myth of positive thinking gives rise to *con*fidence that ultimately fails in the face of sustained adversity and resistance. Positive thinking is incapable of producing reliable confidence because it lacks a true power source. Tozer was right when he wrote, "Our confidence must always be in Christ and His abilities. Whenever we think we can, we usually end up failing miserably."[33]

CHAPTER 5
THE MYTH OF EXPERIENCE

"[God] calls us to trust him so completely that we are unafraid to put ourselves in situations where we will be in trouble if He doesn't come through."
—Francis Chan

Experience goes hand-in-hand with *con*fidence. We seek it because we believe it will open the doors to opportunity. It becomes the building blocks of the resumes we use to showcase our expertise, advance our careers, and garner admiration.

There is a fundamental reality about experience—it's inevitable. But learning from our experience is optional. If we think about our experience without bias, we'll see that we are not as good as our most successful experiences lead us to believe, and we are not as bad as our worst experiences make us feel.

There is a fundamental reality about experience — it's inevitable.

The Myth of Experience

We are looking for confidence in all the wrong places when we pursue and rely on our worldly experience instead of putting our full trust in the Lord.

Ask Me How Good I Am

Marshall Goldsmith is one of the world's preeminent business coaches. Working with Fortune 500 organizations, he asked 50,000 participants in his training programs to rate themselves in terms of their performance compared to their professional peers. The results stunningly reflect how highly we regard our experience and competence—70 percent believed they were in the top 10 percent of their peer group, and 80-85 percent believed they were in the top 20 percent.[34] We see ourselves as top-performers.

It may be hard to accept, but all the research points to the fact that we struggle to see ourselves as we are. I clung to a mental picture of how I wanted people to perceive me. We all do. It's our only honest conclusion. This is why it is so difficult to accept that our past experience does not guarantee future success—or failure. But it most certainly assures we will *confidently* bet on ourselves. Our natural inclination is to rely on our expertise to guide our thinking and decision making. Given we have used our past experience as a successful navigational tool, isn't it reasonable to conclude that we will depend upon it to be a reliable guide for our future?

> Based on our interpretation of our experience, we search for and use evidence that confirms our beliefs about ourselves and how we think the world should operate.

This is the premise of the myth of experience–it's a focusing illusion. Based on our interpretation of our experience, we search for and use evidence that confirms our beliefs about ourselves and how we think the world should operate. It broadly ignores or discounts information that conflicts with our self-assessment.

Operating under the myth of experience, I believed I had reached a place where I was irreplaceable in my career. Most of us do. Unfortunately, there is something deceptively familiar about experience. It makes you feel at home. You know that place where you kick off your shoes, sink into your favorite chair, pour yourself a cold drink, and think you are in a safe place.

Failed by Experience

The problem with relying on the self-assessment of our experience as a guide to life is that it's veiled in *con*fidence. If we were playing baseball and found ourselves standing on third base, we'd conclude we hit a triple—tipping our cap to the cheers of an adoring crowd. We wouldn't think to consider that we might have arrived at this celebrated stature on the wings of good fortune and exceptional circumstances. Instead, we'd embrace the result, ignore the path, and draw deeper into *con*fidence. When our experience keeps us from challenging assumptions, asking penetrating questions, and thinking beyond surface-level appearances, we live under the myth of experience. History is littered with people who failed to finish strong because they trusted their own experience.

> When our experience keeps us from challenging assumptions, asking penetrating questions, and thinking beyond surface-level appearances, we live under the myth of experience.

Consider King Asa

> "In the twentieth year of Jeroboam king of Israel, Asa became king of Judah, and he reigned in Jerusalem forty-one years...Asa did what was right in the eyes of the Lord, as his father David had done."
> —I Kings 15:9 & 11, NIV

Asa did what was right in the eyes of the Lord for the first 36 years of his reign—relying on God for everything. King Asa and the nation of Judah prospered because he honored God in word and deed. Asa won great wars, kept the law and commandments, pointed his people back to God. He even fired his mother because of her stubborn idolatry. You know you are living for God when you willingly terminate your mom's employment.

For 36 years, Asa lived and ruled under the umbrella of God's protection. Now in the twilight of his reign, he had the finish line in sight! He was on his way to finishing strong. Then, in the face of a new challenge, the King decides to rely on his experience's confidence rather than continuing to look to God for strength, answers, and deliverance.

It begins to unravel when Asa decides to empty the national treasury to bribe the Syrians for support. God rewards his poor decision by telling him he will be under the siege of his enemies for the rest of his years. As if that was not enough, Asa fell ill. Again he chose to ignore God's counsel and followed the guidance of his physicians. It took King Asa 36 years to get in position to finish well. But choosing to rely on his experience gave rise to *con*fidence that caused him to stumble and fail.

Failed by Experience

Experience expands our knowledge and builds our expertise. Asa's story demonstrates how experience fills us full of *con*fidence. Throughout history, you repeatedly find that the reliance upon *con*fidence gives rise to two blinding conditions—ignorance and pride. Asa's story is not unique but an eloquent example of why finishing strong is so difficult.

> Throughout history, you repeatedly find that the reliance upon confidence gives rise to two blinding conditions— ignorance and pride.

Experience camouflages a trap—the higher you rise in stature, and the longer you live, the fewer people there are to offer honest feedback or restrain our unpleasant traits. Pride and ignorance keep us from asking for help and seeking wise counsel—opening the trap door to the experience myth.

> "When pride comes, then comes disgrace,
> but with the humble is wisdom."
> —Proverbs 11:2, ESV

Pride leads us to accept our strengths and successes as absolute proof that we possess no weaknesses. Pride goes hand-in-hand with ignorance. I refused to see my pride for the longest time. I recognize it now—stubbornly resisting saying I'm sorry, making decisions in a vacuum, rejecting feedback, discounting wise counsel, ignoring the needs of others, and craving recognition.

The myth of experience says, "I can do all things by gaining competence through experience." The truth about experience is that it's inevitable and insufficient to finish strong because it creates fertile ground where *con*fidence thrives.

We, like Asa, only finish once. We look for confidence in all the wrong places when we pursue and rely on our experience instead of putting our full trust in the Lord.

CHAPTER 6
THE MYTH OF FALSE IDENTITY

"If we find ourselves with a desire that nothing in
this world can satisfy, the most probable explanation
is that we were made for another world."
—C. S. Lewis

Who am I? Who hasn't asked themselves this question? Early in life, we tie our identity to our family, our school, our hobbies, the sports we played, the clubs we belonged to, or maybe where we lived or grew up. If we gained recognition as a student, athlete, or musician, that became our identity and shaped our expectations about the colleges we should attend and careers to pursue. Equally, if we didn't fit in, we tried to run from a painful and lonely identity and create a more inviting one.

Who we are is how people know us. When we meet someone for the first time, what do we do? Exactly, we ask and answer questions about identity. What do you do? Where do you live? Where did you go to school? Tell me about your family? What do you like to do when you are not working? Ask someone any of these questions and you'll get a glimpse into their identity.

We answer these questions based primarily on social cues—how we see ourselves fitting into the world around us. This world-centric view gives rise to the myth of false identity that says, "I am who I am and where I am based on my standing in the world." There is something perpetually unsettling and uncertain about identity found in the world—evidence of the labels we use to frame our identity. We use identity labels to keep score, build up and tear down, inspire greatness, inflict pain, unify, and divide.

> There is something perpetually unsettling and uncertain about identity found in the world — evidence of the labels we use to frame our identity.

The Myth of False Identity

We are looking for confidence in all the wrong places when we look for our identity anywhere other than in Christ.

Mistaken Identity

We crave *con*fidence because we are naturally under-confident—it's part of our fallen nature. Needing a "smart" way to sell the myth of false identity, we frame it as a challenge—"Become the best version of yourself." On this path, we satisfy our appetite for *con*fidence by improving our worldly identity—shed labels that tie us to our failures, pain, and loneliness and secure tags that attract praise, rewards, and standing.

> "Man looks at the outward appearance,
> but the Lord looks at the heart."
> —1 Samuel 16:7, ESV

For me, outward appearances—position, prestige, and possessions—reflected the best version of me. I wasn't always sure where I was going, but there was no mistaking the direction of my heart. The measuring stick I used was being the first or youngest to accomplish milestones. Ultimately, my professional identity was that of a senior-level Fortune 50 executive. This identity, at the time, was the best and most confident version of me.

My identity investment was validated the day I was told I had earned the designation of HP+—"High-Performance Plus." It was an exclusive, high-visibility club. "HP+" signified the executive team believed I possessed the ability to rise to the highest levels of leadership and influence in the organization—even CEO. I loved the notoriety and assignments that came with this label. It boosted my *con*fidence and instilled a false hope that further entangled me in my worldly identity.

When you are brimming with *con*fidence, I can assure you that you don't see the world and your place in it as it truly is—you see it as you perceive yourself. At this point in my life, my identity reflected my career position and standing. So when my career was terminated in the events that unfolded on March 13, 2013, it caught me entirely off guard.

I was sitting in the same hotel where I hosted a celebration of my team's accomplishments a few days earlier. It was surreal being told you were not part of the organization's future going forward in the same place where you had just been thanked and congratulated for your team's performance. Near the end of our brief meeting, I started to ask our CEO about my designation as an HP+. Before I could finish my question, she said, "You were never an HP+ in my mind!" I walked into that meeting *con*fident of who I was. I walked out angry, disappointed, and confused. Without the prestige of my career, who was I now?

> "Let us then with confidence draw near to the throne of grace, that we may receive mercy and find grace to help in time of need."
> —Hebrews 4:16, ESV

My "HP+" designation reflected who I thought I was. It was a false identity, but still, I chose it. It demonstrates the alluring nature of *con*fidence. The enemy is an inclusive *con* man. He targets all of us with his deception. Be sure any identity we seek apart from Christ is a fraud that pushes us down alluring paths that feed our *con*fidence. Struggle and ultimately defeat awaits us if we choose to construct our identity in the world based upon false labels, misplaced priorities, and self-indulgent focus.

> **Be sure any identity we seek apart from Christ is a fraud that pushes us down alluring paths that feed our confidence.**

The Truth About Identity

It doesn't matter to the enemy on which shaky foundation we choose to stand because he's successfully *conned* us into standing on the edge of a crumbling cliff. The enemy's goal is simply to get us to tie our confidence to our worldly identity—good or bad. Either way, it tethers us to one of two ledges. On one ledge, we are a victor seeing ourselves in control—as I did. The other ledge is that of a victim—seeing ourselves as unloved and forgotten.

Jesus said,

> "How can you believe, when you receive glory from one another and do not seek the glory that comes from the only God?"
> —John 5:44, ESV

It was hard for me to wrap my head around the fact that seeking and receiving glory from the world invites chaos into our lives. However, it explained why I felt so frightened and disoriented. Everything that binds us to the world ties our identity and pursuits to titles, celebrity, and prestige—from here, nothing we do will prosper. It may produce a few shining moments that will encourage us along the path. But when we rise on the wings of *con*fidence, our destiny is inevitable failure.

Looking for *con*fidence apart from Christ draws us away from Him—cutting off the source of our strength and most profound purpose. Embracing whose we are first—God's and God's alone—is the only way to correctly identify who we are.

CHAPTER 7
THE MYTH OF MEDIOCRITY

"Souls are like athletes that need opponents worthy
of them, if they are to be tried and extended and
pushed to the full use of their powers."
—Thomas Merton

How would you respond to me, declaring, "My mom makes the best apple pie!" "Prove it," right? My mom baked dozens of "proof pies" to back up my claim over the years.

For years, my friend Dan heard me brag about my mom's apple pies. In what is nothing short of a shameless act of begging, he said to my mom, "Gwen, I heard you make the best apple pie in the world." Soaking these words in as the heart-felt compliment it was intended, my mom replied, "I should make you one."

Mom's amazing pies start with a crust crafted from scratch. She blends the ingredients by hand with a touch of love. Any extra crust is rolled out on a cookie sheet, sprinkled with sugar and cinnamon, and baked until it turns a beautiful golden brown. The resulting masterpiece is flaky, moist, and melts in your mouth. In a matter of minutes, the sweet aroma of baking fills the house. When the pie crust comes out of the oven, don't delay getting to the kitchen because this sweet, flaky treat will be gone.

The day before I was to see Dan, the smell of Mom's pie crust drew me to the kitchen. I knew his apple pie was in the oven. My mouth watered at the sight of the sweet, golden brown, flaky treat sitting on the stovetop. A look of concern on my mom's face stopped me from digging in. "I think something is wrong with my pie crust today. Taste this," she said, as she handed me a piece. One bite was all it took to confirm her fear. "What happened to your pie crust? Did you do something different?" I asked. "Yes," she said, "I used a different brand of flour because it was on sale."

Dan never knew his original apple pie ended up in the trash. That's the only suitable destination for a pie that falls below the Gwen Akers' apple pie standard. I shook my head in disbelief as I dropped it into the garbage can. I have no doubt Dan would have enjoyed the pie—might even have said it was the best he ever tasted. We'll never know because my mom baked a fresh apple pie for Dan. Mixing her recipe-tested flour with her usual touch of love resulted in an apple pie that Dan praised as the best apple pie he had ever had. The standard was met.

The Myth of Mediocrity

We are looking for confidence in all the wrong places when we look anywhere other than to God to set our standards.

> We guard our confidence in mediocrity by setting our standards at the boundary of our perceived confidence rather than looking to the Father to be the standard-bearer.

What's Your Standard?

The myth of mediocrity says if you set your standard at the level that gives you the best chance to be consistently viewed as successful—high or low, you'll possess confidence. We guard our *con*fidence in mediocrity by setting our standards at the boundary of our perceived *con*fidence rather than looking to the Father to be the standard-bearer.

> "For all that is in the world—the desires of the flesh
> and the desires of the eyes and pride in possessions—
> is not from the Father but is from the world."
> —I John 2:16, ESV

Thinking about standards, who set yours? What is your standard? It's easy to slip into mediocrity. We can recognize it by the terms we use to protect our *con*fidence.

- "This is about as good as it gets."
- "No one could reasonably expect more."
- "Pretty good for a kid from…"
- "I'm too young for that assignment…"
- "Better than most."
- "Not that bad considering…"
- "I'm retired now…"
- "God wouldn't use someone like me to…"

I've never met anyone who sets out to be mediocre. It's not God's plan for us. But when we let our desires become the standard-bearer in our lives, we concede control to the enemy—giving him a stronghold that keeps us stuck in *con*fidence.

When we let our desires become the standard-bearer in our lives, we concede control to the enemy — giving him a stronghold that keeps us stuck in confidence.

Achieving performance standards is critical to achieving career success—it's part of the game. A vital element of the game was what we called the annual "budgeting Olympics." In my experience, this was the time for uber-confident leaders to become shamefully weak and shallow as they attempted to gain agreement to the lowest possible standards of performance. Win the gold medal in this competition and you most assuredly maximized the opportunity to earn financial rewards and career advancement for you and your team.

Year by year, I got drawn deeper into the game. Each victory added to my *con*fidence and a belief that I was living under the umbrella of God's blessing. But my standards were set based on worldly cues. My scorecard was simple. Marriage is good, check. Kids are good, check. Pray on the run and at the dinner table, check. Keep my Bible on my nightstand in case of emergencies, check. Attend church on Sunday, check. Volunteer occasionally, check. Give money to God's work, check. Career is thriving, check.

> We are all inclined to determine our own standards because we want to believe we are in control.

I didn't ask God for any help or guidance setting the standards—I decided. I think we are all inclined to determine our own standards because we want to believe we are in control. Therefore, either consciously or by omission, we limit our limitless God. It isn't that the miraculous things God has done through unlikely and unsuspecting people don't amaze us. It is merely where our imagination ends. We struggle to see Him doing incredible or miraculous works through us. So we settle into the comfort of mediocrity.

> God will go to extraordinary lengths to get our attention. He wants us to see that the source of our standard becomes the source of our strength.

By worldly standards, I was living a successful life. Setting my standards to fit comfortably into the world produced the *con*fidence I sought. But as I've described, when adversity struck, my *con*fidence crumbled quickly. I now realize that on that fateful day, Mary didn't end my career—God did. God will go to extraordinary lengths to get our attention. He wants us to see that the source of our standard becomes the source of our strength. There is no lasting strength in *con*fidence.

> He who dwells in the shelter of the Most High
> will abide in the shadow of the Almighty.
> I will say to the Lord, "My refuge and my fortress,
> my God, in whom I trust…"
> For he will command his angels concerning you
> to guard you in all your ways.
> On their hands they will bear you up,
> lest you strike your foot against a stone.
> You will tread on the lion and the adder;
> the young lion and the serpent you will trample underfoot.
> —Psalm 91:1-2, 9-13, CEB

What type of apple pie are you going to bake? God's standards are the best. God wants the best for you. Mediocre is not His standard for your life because it can only produce *con*fidence that will crumble when confronted with adversity. He will go to extraordinary lengths to point out that we need to throw out the apple pies that are not up to His standard.

When we embrace God as the source of our standard, He will become the source of strength. When we rest in the shelter of the Most High, we won't go looking for our confidence in the standards of the world.

CHAPTER 8
THE WILDERNESS MENTALITY

"God tests us to display us. The devil tempts us to destroy us."
—Larry Julian

Wilderness experiences are not high on my list of fun things to do. I am not a hiker, hunter, or fisherman. I am not a swimmer, surfer, or boogie boarder. I lived a few miles from the beautiful beaches of Southern California for 40 years, but I don't like sand in my shoes. I appreciate the beauty and serenity of a secluded golf course but prefer to stay out of the woods. Add the fact that I think the dark is incredibly disorienting (sounds better than saying I'm afraid of the dark) which tells you everything you need to know about my inclination to choose a wilderness experience.

> God aims to use wilderness experiences for our good and to fulfill His purpose.

But life's mental wilderness experiences are different. No one says, "I sure hope God will lead me into the wilderness today." I certainly didn't ask Him to, and I'm sure you don't either. I believe life's wilderness experiences appear as an unwelcome and unannounced visitor from both experience and observation. God aims to use wilderness experiences for our good and to fulfill His purpose. The enemy aims for them to take up permanent residence in our hearts, souls, and minds. In my case, it showed up as the crashing of my career.

Wilderness experiences also show up as divorce, illness, financial problems, failed relationships, betrayal, and/or the loss of a loved one. They'll also press upon our patience and ask you to wait for important news. Did you make the team? Was your application or offer accepted? Is someone you love coming home?

> We lose confidence for all the wrong reasons when we get trapped in a wilderness mentality.

We lose confidence for all the wrong reasons when we get trapped in a wilderness mentality.

Standing in the Wilderness

Can you remember a time when you felt like you were standing in a mental wilderness? Is there a darker or lonelier place to be? It's difficult to see through when you are overwhelmed and disoriented by your surroundings. You're reluctantly thrown into an emotional and intellectual wrestling match that distracts your attention and drains the vital energy you need to mount your escape. Now you're standing at a critical crossroad, surrounded by road signs filled with unanswerable questions.

- Why am I in this place, Lord?
- How could you allow this to happen to me?
- What do you want me to do now?
- Why isn't God answering my prayers?
- What is my purpose now?
- Why won't God tell me what to do next?
- Why didn't you reward me for doing what was right?

Wilderness Mentality

A wilderness mentality is the false belief that God does not care about us and is unaware of our current circumstances. It gives rise to a feeling of abandonment and resignation the enemy uses to push us to give up. In my mind, it sounded like this, "Okay, Lord, I know I screwed up. I admitted it. Did you hear me? I said I give up." We beg, "Come on, enough is enough. Please tell me what lesson you are trying to teach me?" Mentally beaten down, doubt emerges. "If He always hears my prayers, why isn't he answering?" "Lord, if you don't mind, could you please send me a text message that you'll respond later. Please?" We question His love. "If He loves me, why isn't He showing me the way out—the path to healing?" Ultimately, I figured out all I ever had was *con*fidence.

> A wilderness mentality is the false belief that God does not care about us and is unaware of our current circumstances.

Is it even possible to feel confident amid a wilderness experience? I wasn't sure. It's embarrassing to admit you've gone looking for confidence in all the wrong places. You're so busy cursing God you can't see He's seeking you. All the while, the enemy is rejoicing over your wilderness plight. As you push God away, Satan fans the flames of your discontent—encouraging you to challenge everything you know about His love, goodness, and sovereignty.

Be Still

Pushing God aside made my feelings of loneliness grow—chipping away at the moorings of my faith. I didn't want to admit that I was angry with God—do any of us? Standing in a foreign territory, I prayed earnestly to be released from my sentence. I even threw in, "If it is your will," from time to time, thinking this would be the key to ending God's perceived silence.

When you go looking for confidence in all the wrong places, you don't get to dictate the terms of your recovery. I discovered the path out of the wilderness begins with silence.

> "Be quick to listen, slow to speak, and slow to grow angry."
> —James 1:19

I never took this instruction seriously. Only in silence did I begin to understand if we don't give God room to speak and work in our lives, He'll feel more distant and unresponsive to us. Many mornings I sat in silence. There is something uniquely beautiful and peaceful about silently pursuing God. It ultimately allowed me to rest in the promise:

> "And we know that for those who love God all
> things work together for good for those who
> are called according to his purpose."
> —Romans 8:28

Wilderness experiences are vital for training our faith. "We walk by faith, not by sight" (2 Corinthians 5:7, ESV). The enemy attacks our vulnerability in the wilderness. He seizes the moment as an opportunity to destroy our relationship with God—pushing us to question our eternal destiny. The enemy loves to nurture our wilderness mentality because it moves us toward greater self-reliance.

Understanding the Wilderness

Julian of Norwich wrote the earliest surviving book in the English language to be written by a woman, *Revelations of Divine Love*. When she found herself amid a wilderness experience, she declared, "In God's sight we do not fall: in our own we do not stand…God loved us before he made us; and his love has never diminished and never shall." There is only one path out of the wilderness—pursuing an intimate relationship with Jesus Christ. "For everyone who has been born of God overcomes the world. And this the victory that has overcome the world—our faith" (I John 5:4, ESV). We cannot avoid the wilderness, but we do not have to fear it.

To put wilderness experiences in perspective, consider that the Israelites turned an 11-day journey into 40 years of wandering. I draw two conclusions from this fact. First, it should make any wandering assignment we receive seem trite. Second, our wilderness experiences are purposeful. We delay God's prescriptive lesson when we choose our plans over His. When you think you have a better way and ignore His invitation to the banquet hall of eternity, prepare yourself for an extended stay in the wilderness.

There is only one path out of the wilderness — pursuing an intimate relationship with Jesus Christ.

> "And a highway will be there; it will be called the Way of Holiness; it will be for those who walk on that Way. The unclean will not journey on it; wicked fools will not go about on it."
> —Isaiah 35:8, NIV

We lose confidence for all the wrong reasons when we get trapped in a wilderness mentality. There is no denying that wilderness assignments will be challenging, unwelcome, and undesirable, but we are not alone. "Be glad in the Lord always! Again I say, be glad," (Philippians 4:4, NIV), our God is continually preparing us to fulfill His higher purpose.

CHAPTER 9
TIMELESS MEANS TIMELESS

"God has not called me to be successful.
He called me to be faithful."
—Mother Teresa

Legend has it that a man was lost in the desert and had exhausted all of his supplies. In desperate need of water and shade, he was overjoyed to come upon a dilapidated shack. As he sat down in the shade of the shack his eyes were immediately drawn to a rusty hand-crank water pump. He stumbled over to it, grabbed the handle, and vigorously pumped the handle up and down to no avail—not a single drop of water.

Surveying the area around the pump, he noticed an old jug. He picked it up and rubbed away the crusted dirt to discover a message scratched into its side. It read, "You have to prime the pump with all the water in this jug, my friend. P. S. Be sure to refill the jug and secure the cork tightly before you leave."

Given what he thought was a dry well, he was surprised to find the jug full of water when he popped its cork off. He was overjoyed to see the water, but it presented him with a life and death decision—drink the water and live or prime the pump and take a chance on producing an abundance of water. Observing the fragile condition of the jug and pump, he struggled to believe that priming the pump was the right choice.

After considering those who might follow him, he hesitantly poured all the water into the top of the pump and slowly started cranking the handle up and down. The pump squeaked with each stroke, but there still was no sign of water! Fearing he had made a big mistake, a wave of panic swept over him. Just as he was about to give up, a few dribbles of rusty water dripped to the ground. Encouraged by the sight of the drips, he pumped harder and faster—the rusty dribble quickly became a gushing stream of cool, clean water.

Now water flowed abundantly. The man repeatedly filled the jug and splashed cool water on his face. With every refreshing sip, he thought about the message on the jug, "What if I wouldn't have trusted the message?" Before continuing his journey, he filled the jug to the brim and sealed it tightly with the cork. Then he found a sharp rock and scratched, "P.S.S. I promise you this works. If you pour it all in, you'll get it all back and more."

> We lose confidence for all the wrong reasons when we fail to claim God's promises. Biblical truths don't cease to be true because we don't know them or ignore them.

We lose confidence for all the wrong reasons when we fail to claim God's promises. Biblical truths don't cease to be true because we don't know them or ignore them.

A Promise is a Promise

Would you have primed the pump—acted on the promise inscribed on the jug? A promise is "a declaration or assurance that one will do a particular thing or that particular thing will happen."[35] Wouldn't you agree the man took a big risk? He had no idea who wrote the message on the bottle, when the last time someone successfully primed the pump, or if the well still contained water. He had every reason to question the promise and promise giver. Let's not fool ourselves, we do it all the time.

The enemy wants you to believe there's no water in the jug. He wants you to believe the Bible is like that old jug and the old pump is sunk into a dry well. He wants you to believe you need to drink the water or you will die. He wants you to question the promise and the promise giver so you will be forever limited to his *con*fidence.

Timeless Means Timeless

Did you know there are more than 7,000 promises in Scripture?[36] God—our Promise Giver—guarantees the fulfillment of every one of them. His performance track record is perfect—fulfilling His every promise and prophecy. That's what makes God's promises unique and wonderful—they are timeless. Every promise is neither time stamped nor affected by the passage of time. When I say, "Timeless means timeless," I am reminding you that God's promises are lasting, enduring, permanent, and eternal.

We lose confidence for all the wrong reasons when we don't know God's promises because we can't claim what we don't know. So when adversity strikes, if we are unable to rest in the strength of God's promises, fear breaks us down. Think of fear as a misunderstanding of who God is [His nature] and what He has promised [His character].[37] God has been good and He will continue to fulfill His promises regardless of what we experience transpiring in the world around us.

> **Confidence is opposed to God's promises—a comparison of what is finite to He who is infinite, infallible, and omnipotent.**

*Con*fidence is opposed to God's promises—a comparison of what is finite to He who is infinite, infallible, and omnipotent. In *con*fidence, our impact and contribution are limited to what can be done in our strength and within our resources. People who don't know God's promises live in limited and unreliable *con*fidence because they:

- Fear failure
- Fear success

- Believe they are not good enough
- Define temporary circumstances as permanent conditions
- Fear the unknown
- Think God wouldn't give them a big assignment
- Choose scarcity over abundance
- Seek to be served before serving
- Believe God's promises are situational

The timeless nature of God's promises means we have access to the strength, hope, and resources we need to answer every question, need, or problem we face in life. When we falsely believe that God's promises are situational or have an expiration date, we are subject to losing our confidence for all the wrong reasons.

It's Easy to Claim God's Promises

A Sunday school teacher gave her young students an assignment to claim God's protection and strength by memorizing the 23rd Psalm. You are likely familiar with it, but it is so rich and beautiful it is always good to be reminded.

> The Lord is my shepherd, I lack nothing.
> He makes me lie down in green pastures,
> he leads me beside quiet waters,
> he refreshes my soul.
> He guides me along the right paths
> for his name's sake.
> Even though I walk
> through the darkest valley,
> I will fear no evil,
> for you are with me;

> your rod and your staff,
> they comfort me.
> You prepare a table before me
> in the presence of my enemies.
>
> You anoint my head with oil;
> my cup overflows.
> Surely your goodness and love will follow me
> all the days of my life,
> and I will dwell in the house of the Lord
> forever.
> —Psalm 23, NIV

She told them that they would have the opportunity to recite it at the end of the month at a Sunday service. One of her students, excited about the assignment, practiced every day. When his turn came to claim God's promise as his own and share it with the congregation, he was overcome with nerves. So he closed his eyes and took a couple of deep breaths. With his eyes still closed, he began, "The Lord is my shepherd," then opened his eyes. Seeing all the people, he froze. Trying to regain his focus, he took a couple deep breaths. Again he proudly announced to the congregation, "The Lord is my shepherd." After a momentary pause, he continued, "And that's all you really need to know."

We lose confidence for all the wrong reasons when we get conned into thinking what lies before us exceeds the breadth and depth of God's promises.

It is that simple. All you really need to know is that God's promises are timeless. We lose confidence for all the wrong reasons when we get *conned* into thinking what lies before us exceeds the breadth and depth of God's promises.

> "…this is my prayer. That God, the God of our Lord Jesus Christ and the all-glorious Father, will give you spiritual wisdom and the insight to know more of him: that you may receive that inner illumination of the spirit which

will make you realize how great is the hope to which he is calling you—the magnificence and splendor of the inheritance promised to Christians—and how tremendous is the power available to us who believe in God."
—Ephesians 1:18-19, PHILLIPS

CHAPTER 10
BAD THINGS DO HAPPEN TO GOOD PEOPLE

"Even when things are hard, let my deep love for you remind you that I will be there to help you through it."
—Isaiah 43:2

"He's a good ol' boy." My Dad would say this with a wry smile on his face. I laugh every time I hear these words. It's a down-home Southern saying. He was referring to someone he found to be honest, trustworthy, and authentic—just like my dad. Today, we might say, "He/She is good people."

John Kolendich was good people—"A good ol' boy," for sure. John loved his family and cherished his friends. You would've loved John. Unfortunately, we didn't get to love him long enough. John lost a courageous battle with throat cancer on September 22, 2003. I lost something that day. It made me wonder, "Why do bad things happen to good people?"

Not long before John died, he asked me if I would help his wife Kathleen and their three kids Johnny (10), Nicholas (9), and Katherine (4) if he did not beat his cancer. It was a request that I prayed would never have to be honored. Ten weeks later, while still working through the grief of John's passing, my Dad passed away on December 3. My Dad was a good ol' boy; you would have loved my dad too—everyone did.

Losing my Dad and John shook me. I'm sure you've wrestled with the same feelings. What I've come to know is we lose confidence for all the wrong reasons when we forget that God is still present and at work writing His redemptive story when bad things happen to good people.

Bad Things Do Happen

How do you respond when bad things happen to good people? Suppose you are not connected in some way to the story. In that case, you'll likely be unaffected—easily ignore the unexplainable pain and grief. But what if you are part of the story? Now, it's no longer simply news. It's personal—objectively senseless to you. Thus, the insulation that guards your emotions gets stripped away—exposing pain and grief that can't be explained.

When we can't make sense of the bad things that happen to the good people in our lives or to us, it can invoke what psychologists call "below the line" thinking. It's a mindset that locks you into the belief that there has to be a reasonable explanation for what has happened. So, we create our own cause by assigning fault to someone or something. "Below the line" thinking exposes the frailty of *confidence*—erecting a victim's mentality. Thinking like a victim leads us to question our faith, seek consolation in the wrong places, make decisions based on false conclusions, and ultimately lose confidence for the wrong reasons.

Did you know, "Words like trials, temptations, refining, and testing occur more than 200 times in the Bible?"[38] These are common life experiences and can happen at any time. Bad things appear in our lives as:

- Trials: unexpected challenges that disrupt our lives without warning.
- Physical challenges: illness and injuries.
- Rejection: being turned down or away from someone or something we love.
- Persecution: needing to stand alone when our faith is challenged.
- Detours and disappointments: hardship inflicted by being taken off our intended course.
- Temptation: making a choice that yields to our nature and produces an avoidable burden.

Why, or What?

It can be binding if it paralyzes us. In the enemy's hands, we ask, "Why?" "Why is this happening to me?" "Why?" is a question asked out of weakness, which binds us to our pain. Resting in the Father's hands, we ask, "What?" "What good are you going to do through this suffering, and what do you want me to do next?" The power in asking "What" is that it points us towards the hope we have in Christ.

The power in asking "What" is that it points us towards the hope we have in Christ.

"Every good gift, every perfect gift, comes from above. These gifts come down from the Father, the creator of the heavenly lights, in whose character there is no change at all."
—James 1:17, CEB

The enemy wants us to get stuck on asking, "Why," when bad things happen. Because as long as we are stuck on trying to understand something that can never make sense to us in our own wisdom, we construct a barrier that blocks us from experiencing God's peace. God is not the author of pain and suffering. He will allow it to enter our lives, but He is not required to give us an explanation. Even if God readily gave us an answer, it doesn't change our condition. We can defiantly refuse to accept God's providence. Still, He will not adjust to our wishes, sense of justice, or demands. He is going to keep on being God.

Who's in Your Boat?

When bad things happen, it is not a reason for us to lose confidence. We see a perfect example of this after Jesus fed the five thousand (Mark 6:30-56). As Jesus dismissed the crowds, He "made His disciples get into the boat and go before Him to the other side, to Bethsaida," while He went to pray.

The winds were blowing so hard against them; they were making little progress. After straining for a few hours, can you imagine their frustration? They were experienced fishermen, so the disciples likely thought they should never have gotten in the boat to make this journey. Can you feel them getting more irritated with Jesus with every excruciating stroke of their oars? They might even have wondered aloud, "Where is He in the midst of this storm?" So it is with us—in the midst of life's storms, we lose confidence because we falsely believe God has abandoned us.

> In the midst of life's storms, we lose confidence because we falsely believe God has abandoned us.

We are told they are in the fourth watch of the night, which means they had been struggling against the wind for as many as twelve hours when Jesus "came to them, walking on the sea." Get a good picture of this. Jesus is purposefully walking towards Bethsaida. In fact, "He meant to pass by them." Yes, pass them by, "but when they saw him walking on the sea they thought it was a ghost, and cried out, for they all saw Him and were terrified."

What happens next is significant. Jesus announces the reason they should be courageous at this moment. "But immediately He spoke to them and said, 'Take heart; it is I. Do not be afraid.'" Why should we seek refuge in Christ? Because of what Jesus does next, "And He got into the boat with them, and the wind ceased."

We lose confidence for all the wrong reasons when we interpret the terrible things that happen to good people as a sign that Jesus is not going to accept our invitation to get in our boat and calm the storms. *Con*fidence assuredly will fail us during the storms of life. People we trusted and loved will abandon us. Unforeseen circumstances will rob our health, finances, and joy. But God has not forgotten us. He is aware of every storm and has a purpose for it.

God's Character

I miss my dad and John. Beyond the personal loss of friendship and wisdom, their passing changed the course of my career. Because I was no longer willing to move to a new location, I turned down promotions. Ultimately they stopped offering them. So, I indeed asked God why He took them from us. I also asked God why He ended my career. Having already accepted less than I had hoped for and dreamed, why did He terminate it? This pushed me deep into the "below the line" thinking.

> Sometimes God will allow something unexpected and unwelcome to enter our lives. But it is not without purpose.

We lose confidence for all the wrong reasons when we lose sight that God is still God—sovereign and providential when bad things happen to good people. Sometimes God will allow something unexpected and unwelcome to enter our lives. But it is not without purpose. "God is a Spirit, infinite, eternal, and unchangeable in His being, wisdom, power, holiness, justice, goodness, and truth."[39] His plan is perfect. We have forgotten who God is if we lose confidence when bad things happen. God's character is perfect—giving us every reason to remain hopeful and resilient regardless of what happens to us or is swirling around us.

> "I know that you can do all things, and that
> no purpose of yours can be thwarted."
> —Job 42:2, ESV

CHAPTER 11
HEY, YOU'RE DRIFTING

"Yet we must be watchful, especially in the beginning of temptation, for the enemy is more easily overcome in the beginning if he is not allowed to enter the door or our hearts, but is resisted outside the gate, at his first knock. When he is not resisted, little by little, he gets complete entrance."
—Thomas à Kempis

On August 9, 1974, Richard M. Nixon resigned from office as the President of the United States for his involvement in the Watergate scandal. Eight days later, Jeb Magruder became the second official of the Nixon administration to plead guilty for his involvement in Watergate.[40]

At his sentencing, Magruder said to Judge John Sirica, "I know what I have done, and Your Honor knows what I have done. Somewhere between my ambition and my ideals, I lost my ethical compass."[41] Somewhere along the course of Jeb Magruder's journey to the finish line, he drifted. You can't help

> None of us wake up in the morning and say, "I think it's a good day to start drifting."

but wonder, how does such a grave failure start? It's deceptively simple; you take what you think is an innocent and non-consequential step and you are on your way.

None of us wake up in the morning and say, "I think it's a good day to start drifting." Equally, temptation doesn't wait for an invitation. It persistently leans on our weaknesses and insecurities—drawing us away from our spiritual, moral, and ethical home. But once we've accepted temptation's invitation, the drifting begins. At first, a warning goes off in our head. But our nature is to silence it with self-justification so we can feel good about who we are, what we believe, and what we are doing. All the time, not recognizing we're adrift—duped by *con*fidence.

> We lose confidence for all the wrong reasons when we drift apart from God's Word—His divine plan and purpose for our lives.

We lose confidence for all the wrong reasons when we drift apart from God's Word—His divine plan and purpose for our lives.

Where Does Drifting Start?

I can relate to Jeb Magruder. I wish I couldn't. But it's my nature. Sorry, but it's yours too. If you can't connect with Jeb Magruder, you are in denial. I don't like to hear or use the word "sin" because it cuts through attempts at self-justification and exposes the heart and soul of who I am—who we all are. When we ignore the threat of temptation and the nature of sin, our moral compass starts spinning. We lose our sense of direction and start drifting away into enemy territory—apart from God's guidance and protection. Paul points this out to us, writing,

> "If we say we have no sin, we deceive ourselves, and the truth is not in us."
> —1 John 1:8, ESV

Deception (temptation), doubt, discouragement, disappointment, defeat, disaster, downfall, disbelief, distrust, decline, detachment, despair, disillusion, and divorce are the "D-words" that serve to untether us from God. In *The Screwtape Letters*, C. S. Lewis highlights how to unlock the "D-words" in an interaction between Screwtape, a senior demon and instructor, and his student Wormwood:

"You will say that these are very small sins; and doubtless, like all young tempters, you are anxious to be able to report spectacular wickedness. But do remember, the only thing that matters is the extent to which you separate the man from the Enemy [God]. It does not matter how small the sins are provided that their cumulative effect is to edge the man away from the Light and out into the Nothing…Indeed the safest road to Hell is the gradual one—the gentle slope, soft underfoot, without sudden turnings, without milestones, without signposts."[42]

Off the Rails

Ruth Graham, Billy and Ruth's third of five children, began drifting after the first of three divorces. Being the daughter of Dr. Billy Graham, arguably the most famous evangelist of the 20th century, meant that Ruth lived in the bright light of unforgiving public opinion. When asked about her first divorce after 18 years of marriage, she said, "I divorced my first husband for years of infidelity, and I was the first one to get a divorce in my family, so that was not good. His parents were friends of the family, so that made it very complicated, and I felt like a circle had been drawn, and I was on the outside of the circle."

Ruth remarried quickly after thinking she found love again. Her new husband threatened Ruth with physical abuse. Not being the man Ruth thought he was, she found herself divorced for a second time. She had nowhere to go, so she decided to return home where she would be met by the man that was not only her father but an icon of the Christian faith.

"My fears multiplied with every mile," she said, adding, "it wasn't just a matter of what my parents would soon say but the example I was making for my children." Fighting back her tears, she continued, "My father was standing there, and when I got out of the car, he wrapped his arms around me and said, 'Welcome home,' and there was never any condemnation."

In her book, *In Every Pew Sits a Broken Heart*, Ruth acknowledged the pain in her life was staggering. "I sort of went off the rails," she wrote. "I decided I was tired of doing it God's way. But that just made things worse. I had thought I was doing everything perfectly. I was a good wife. I was a wonderful mother. I was active in the church and I was teaching Bible studies. So, why didn't God take care of me? The story is not over. But that's OK, God gives me grace. And God is a covenant-keeping God. He is faithful even when I am not. Now I'm living life. I am just living in the grace of God…I finally decided that I was going to admit that I don't have it all together—but God does."[43]

Ruth said, "I remember one day when I was really beating myself up and taking responsibility for my marriage falling apart—just pouring my heart out. Daddy said, 'Quit beating yourself up. We all live under God's grace and we just do the best we can.' Whenever I go home, there's always a bouquet of flowers in my room with a handwritten note that reads, 'Welcome home, Daddy.'"[44]

> Pride acts like a magnet that jumbles our compass. It grows strong in the fertile soil of confidence. Drawn into pursuing our own agenda and rejecting wise counsel, it's not long before we've drifted away from God and His love for us.

I can relate to Ruth Graham's drifting journey. I had to eat a slice of humble pie before admitting I was off the rails and didn't have it all together. Pride acts like a magnet that jumbles our compass. It grows strong in the fertile soil of *con*fidence. Drawn into pursuing our own agenda and rejecting wise counsel, it's not long before we've drifted away from God and His love for us.

Pay Closer Attention

> "Therefore we must pay much closer attention to what we have heard, lest we drift away from it."
> —Hebrews 2:1, ESV

Drifting is the fruit of neglect. It has recognizable symptoms. Screwtape gives us the enemy's script: "It's a gradual one, a gentle slope, soft underfoot and without sudden turnings." He's pointing out the subtlety of drifting. We begin to believe the messages of the world, which desensitize us to the truth. When we no longer see God as the moral lawgiver and the standard of truth, we're susceptible to that danger of seeing the world as we want it to be—a place of fulfillment where our deepest desires and longings can be fulfilled.

I followed the script despite the numerous warning signs along the way. We are drifting away from the safe harbor of God's protection when we:

- Stop pursuing God—pulling away from worship, pushing God's word aside, and failing to seek Him in prayer daily.
- Start losing interest in the goals and dreams God places on our hearts.
- Lose hope during life's storms and allow our minds to dwell in doubt.
- Withdraw from people and the pursuits that previously bolstered our pursuit of God.
- Allow bad habits and routines to take hold of our life.
- Make the pursuit of power, possessions, and prestige our primary focus.

- Push God's grace aside and get consumed by the guilt of our sin(s).
- Seek to fit God into the world. Seeing Him and sharing Him as we want Him to be rather than as He is.

We all drift. None of us have it all together all of the time. *Con*fidence aims to separate us from the work Jesus did on the Cross, but we are never too far from home.

"Nothing can separate us from the love of Christ! We are more than conquerors through him who loved us."
—Romans 8:35-38, ESV

We lose confidence for all the wrong reasons, when we think we have drifted beyond God's redeeming grace.

CHAPTER 12
BLURRY VISION — SPIRITUAL BLINDNESS

"Vision is a God-given burden to see what a person, a place or a situation could become if the grace of God and the power of God were unleashed on them."
—Chip Ingram

For weeks after walking out of my meeting with Mary, I didn't know who I was or where I was going. I am pretty sure shaving every morning kept my wife from being too concerned. Given our history together, growing facial hair screams, "Intervention." If she had known what was churning within me, she would have known my purposeful vision was now blurry at best.

> Immersed in our busy lives, we grow blind to the fact our eyes have wandered away from the Lord.

Even though I saw my leadership role in the organization as indispensable, the reality was different. I was delusional. If you think you aren't dispensable, I'm sorry to break the news to you, but we all are. *Con*fidence blurs our spiritual vision and keeps us from recognizing we've fixed our eyes on worldly targets.

Immersed in our busy lives, we grow blind to the fact our eyes have wandered away from the Lord.

> "Your eye is the lamp of your body. When your eye is healthy, your whole body is full of light, but when it is bad, your body is full of darkness. Therefore be careful lest the light in you be darkness."
> —Luke 11:34–35, ESV

Let me paint you a word picture. Picture your hand submerged in a bucket of water. Now imagine pulling it out quickly. See how fast the water fills in behind your exiting hand? Take a snapshot of this picture and frame it in your mind. Look closely—it's as if your hand was never in the water. Now, how important are you? How busy and engaged are you? What do you think of your plans now?

> We lose confidence for all the wrong reasons when we set our eyes upon gaining honor and position in the world—putting it above a deeper relationship with God.

We lose confidence for all the wrong reasons when we set our eyes upon gaining honor and position in the world—putting it above a deeper relationship with God.

Pulling My Hand Out of the Bucket

I fixed my eyes on my job for nearly 30 years. I pursued it with vigor because I wanted the prestige, rewards, and power that went along with it. It was who I was in the world, and it was the path upon which my *con*fidence was nurtured.

I didn't want to pull my hand out of the bucket. If it weren't for my *con*fidence, I would've seen the problem lying on the horizon. By the time I recognized what was going on, I was immersed in a competition that I could not win. Staring at my hand suspended above the water left no doubt that my career was over. The imagery of pulling my hand out of the bucket of water confronted me with the fact that *con*fidence had failed me. In the eyes of the people I tried so hard to impress, I wasn't that big of a deal after all. The influence and impact I craved and thrived upon were gone as soon as the last ripple from my dripping hand came to rest.

Near or Far-Sighted?

Clinging to our preferences to live for what we think is essential today blurs our vision, hindering our ability to accurately see our eternal finish line. Have you ever locked your eyes on something for a long time, and then when you looked away, everything appeared blurry? Our eyes don't immediately adjust. It takes a few hard blinks to get your eyes to calibrate and produce a clear picture.

*Con*fidence perpetually blurs our vision because it grows from persistently focusing our eyes on worldly pursuits and gaining favor with people. When we hold on to our world-centric vision for our lives, it guarantees God's larger purpose for us will be perpetually out of focus. The lesson here is that near-sighted focus will eventually collide with God's far-sighted vision for our lives. Our goal is not to live well for today, but to finish strong—complete whatever He has uniquely assigned us to do.

In the 9th chapter of John, Jesus heals a blind man. The Pharisees who investigate the healing do not want to believe the man's testimony about Jesus. They are outraged and throw him out into the street. Jesus finds the man and asks, "Do you believe in the son of man?" He answered, 'And who is he, sir, that I may believe in him?' Jesus said to him, 'You have seen him, and it is he who is speaking to you.' He said, 'Lord, I believe,' and he worshiped him." (John 9:35-38, ESV).

Blurry vision is not a reason to lose confidence because it is self-inflicted. It is an indication of reliance on our physical eyes, which are fixed on the world. Divine vision requires eyes of faith—a spiritual focus that ignites our hope in Christ. Jesus finishes by telling the man, "I entered this world to render judgment—to give sight to the blind and to show those who think they see that they are blind" (John 9:39, ESV). Jesus gives us the prescription to curing blurry vision—fix our eyes on Him.

> **Divine vision requires eyes of faith — a spiritual focus that ignites our hope in Christ.**

Spiritual Vision

> "For with you is the fountain of life;
> in your light do we see light."
> —Psalm 36:9, ESV

"Vision is more powerful than sight." These profound words, being uttered by a blind man, sparked my curiosity. What could Henry Wanyoike possibly know about vision? At the age of 21, Henry was blinded by a mild stroke. Before the stroke occurred, he was a promising distance runner with Olympic potential.

At a depth of despair, Henry enrolled in the Machoakos Technical Institute for the Blind. When he arrived, the school's vice principal encouraged Henry to try running again. But he was "so afraid" Henry wasn't inclined to try again. Eventually, with the aid of sighted runners, Henry started to jog. Despite falling a lot, at first, it rekindled Henry's desire to run.

In 2000, he pulled his guide through the final 200 meters to win the gold medal in the 5000 meters at the Sydney Paralympic Games. His winning time was just three seconds off the world record for a blind athlete.[45] Eighteen months later, with the help of his boyhood friend, Joseph Kibunja, they crushed the world record in both the 5000 and 10000 meters at the 2002 World Championships. In 2005, they set a new world record time for the marathon at 2:32:51. The two best friends would best this world record by 80 seconds, one week later, at the Hamburg Marathon.

> Our circumstances can blur our vision — keeping us from seeing God's assignment for our lives. Spiritual vision gives us eyes to see the dreams God places on our hearts.

Without his record-setting feats, it's unlikely anyone would know anything about Henry Wanyoike's life. But Henry never envisioned setting records. When he reached the end of himself, God turned his despair into a dream to positively shape the future of young men and women challenged with physical limitations. Henry is right—"Vision is more powerful than sight." Our circumstances can blur our vision—keeping us from seeing God's assignment for our lives. Spiritual vision gives us eyes to see the dreams God places on our hearts.

Set your eyes on God

Blurry vision is not a reason to lose confidence. "But this is precisely what is written: God has prepared things for those who love him that no eye has seen, or ear has heard, or that haven't crossed the mind of any human being" (1 Corinthians 2:9-10, CEB).

Paul is writing about God's promise to you and me. He starts by reminding us that we can't see what God sees. Just pause for a moment and consider the fact that no eye has seen what God has prepared for you to do. The enemy schemes to blur our vision because it causes us to lose our confidence for all the wrong reasons. When we adhere to God's instruction [keep our eyes fixed on His preferences and priorities for our lives], we will know genuine happiness.[46]

It's always a good time to raise our eyes to Him—fix our gaze upon the Lord our God.

PART THREE
THE SOLUTION
FIVE BUILDING BLOCKS FOR BUILDING THE RELIABLE CONFIDENCE YOU NEED FOR FINISHING STRONG

YOFO—you only finish once! We need to be reminded that most people don't finish strong because they get drawn into the world, which disconnects us from God. Apart from God, our human eyes look for confidence in all the wrong places and lose confidence for all the wrong reasons.

You are God's unique creation. Why should we be Godfident—God-confident about the future? Because he has ordained every step of your life and in every season and circumstance of life is using it to prepare you to do a great work. Paul reminds us of this fact in his letter to the Ephesians, "For we are God's handiwork, created in Christ Jesus to do good works, which God prepared in advance for us to do" (Ephesians 2:10, NIV).

The path to finishing strong is paved with Godfidence. In this section, we will explore how to breathe Godfidence in with every breath you take. The best way to demonstrate the power and importance of cultivating Godfidence in your life is to tell you a story that only makes sense when you get to the end.

How To Finish Strong

Adam's fall was hard and nearly fatal. Confident was one word everyone who knew Adam growing up would use to describe him. He was a good ol' boy—an exemplary young man, a great friend, a straight-A student, and a star football player.

Reunited with an old girlfriend, Adam fell prey to her encouragement to try crack cocaine. One hit and he was hooked. His addiction set his moral compass spinning. Adam betrayed his friends and family—stealing their trust and anything he could turn into cash to feed his destructive habit.

Adam hit rock bottom after his parents handed him over to the County Sheriff and refused to bail him out—he had come to the end of himself. At the request of his parents, Pastor Mike Smith visited Adam in jail. Adam asked the pastor to help him recommit his life to Jesus. Pastor Smith told Adam, "I've been here before with other people in jail. They've prayed like we're about to, but Adam, I want you to know that God can and really does want to change your life. But it begins with an honest and open desire from you to say, 'God, no more is it about me; it's about you.' Are you ready for that commitment?"[47]

This was the first step on Adam's journey to Godfidence. It wasn't easy. The court ordered him to attend a one-year rehab program. It was there he met Kelley, a devoted follower of Christ, who would soon become his wife. He returned home after the completion of the program and the demons of addiction returned too. Adam would disappear, Kelley would find him in a crack house, and Adam would beg her to stay by promising to remain clean. But it was a promise he simply could not keep, which was crushing Kelley's spirit and love for him.

When Kelley threatened to leave Adam, he knew he needed to take drastic measures and began pondering the idea of joining the Navy. Given Adam's history of drugs and theft, the recruiter asked Adam, "Do you really think you can join the Navy? This isn't a joke?"[48] Adam insisted the recruiter call a family friend, who happened to be the highest-ranking recruiting officer in the region. He put his career on the line by telling the recruiter to accept Adam's enlistment.

Adam Brown became the most decorated Navy SEAL in history. Adam's remarkable story is recounted by Eric Blehm in his book *Fearless*. By definition, fearlessness is a state of total confidence. Adam Brown is a poster boy for Godfidence. In his own *con*fidence, Adam nearly lost his wife, family, and life. But under the shield, protection and reliability of Godfidence, he began to live a fearless life.

God became the sole source of Adam's courage and strength. He lived in total Godfidence because he knew there was nothing in this world capable of crowding out God's grace and the power of His promises. Adam spoke openly about the *con*fidence that chided him into believing he was stronger than drug addiction and guided him to betray the trust of his family and friends.

On March 17, 2010, Adam Brown spoke his last words, "I'm okay. I'm okay." Under the umbrella of Godfidence, Adam was always okay. God prospered him and strengthened him despite the loss of his left eye, the loss of fingers on his right hand, surgery on both ankles, a broken leg, the pain of arthritis, and a fragile back. Nothing had stopped Adam until he was caught in a firestorm of enemy bullets on a treacherous mission in Afghanistan. Adam's fellow SEALs saw him as a hero, while he saw himself as a lost and broken soul redeemed by the blood of Jesus Christ.

> **Adam's fellow SEALs saw him as a hero, while he saw himself as a lost and broken soul redeemed by the blood of Jesus Christ.**

His SEAL team risked everything to rescue Adam. They miraculously and heroically exited the mission without a casualty. They encouraged Adam to hang on as their helicopter flew to safety. Adam was rushed into surgery, but it wasn't long before the chilling words, "Adam didn't make it" sounded from their radios.

Adam Brown walked alongside death every day, but he didn't fear it. During his initial combat deployment in Iraq, Adam wrote a letter to his children—Nathan and Savannah. It was a letter Kelley was to read to them in the event Adam did not return home from a mission. Adam wrote, "I'm not afraid of anything that might happen to me on this Earth because I know no matter what, nothing can take my spirit from me…No matter what, my spirit is given to the Lord and I will finally be victorious."[49]

> "I'm not afraid of anything that might happen to me on this Earth because I know no matter what, nothing can take my spirit from me…No matter what, my spirit is given to the Lord and I will finally be victorious."

Godfidence enabled Adam's fearlessness and he wanted everyone to know the source of his courage. He wrote out specific instructions about what he wanted to be said at his funeral—his complete story, including "my life before I met Jesus Christ and Kelley." When Chaplain Springer spoke to the hundreds of people who gathered to celebrate Adam's life, he honored Adam's request—the bad, the worse, the better, and the best. Chaplain Springer told those gathered, "The Gospel was the one thing that gave Adam comfort and hope[50]…Adam surrendered only once, and that was to Jesus Christ."[51] It was in Christ that he came to understand how to serve his SEAL buddies, country, family and friends. You only finish once and Adam Brown finished strong.

Austin Michaels, one of Adam and Kelley's dearest friends, said, "He must have known he'd be a hero if he were killed in action, but he gave the go-ahead to humble himself, to let the world see those skeletons in his closet, to share his testimony."[52]

You Only Finish Once

In Part Three, we'll learn how to be fearless. There are five building blocks for Godfidence.

- The Process—Recalculating—Fix Your Eyes On Jesus

- The Invitation—What Do We Do With Jesus' Invitation?
- Uncovering Purpose—Our Identity in Christ—Purposeful and Powerful
- A Promise is a Promise—Leaning on the Promise Maker
- Dressing the Part—Putting on The Armor of Christ

"May the God of hope fill you with all joy and peace as you trust in Him, so that you may overflow with hope by the power of the Holy Spirit."
—Romans 15:13, NIV

CHAPTER 13
THE PROCESS RECALCULATING — FIX YOUR EYES ON JESUS

"Only in the Cross of Christ will we receive power when we are powerless. We will find strength when we are weak. We will experience hope when our situation is hopeless. Only in the Cross is there peace for our troubled hearts."
—Michael Youssef

"Recalculating, recalculating," you can't stop it. That annoying voice popping out of the dashboard of your car drones on after you failed to execute the navigation system's instructions. The Merriam-Webster dictionary defines recalculating as "The act of calculating again."[53] Okay, credit to Merriam-Webster for precision. Still, it feels like there is an essential element of emotion missing from their definition. The Urban Dictionary's definition of recalculating, "You screwed up, idiot, try it again,"[54] feels more honestly human because we don't like to admit we're lost. We're *con*fident we know where we are going right up to the point we run into a dead end.

Because God created us for Himself, He designed us with an internal navigation system—a spiritual compass—that consistently directs us back to Him. It recognizes when we've made a wrong turn and pings us with the recalculating alert that leads us back to Him. If we don't respond, He seeks us out. It's who He is. It's been that way from the beginning.

> "But the Lord God called to the man and said to him, 'Where are you?'"
> —Genesis 3:9, ESV

Hearing and responding to God's voice is where uncovering the Godfidence necessary to finish strong begins.

Prove It!

After a couple years away at college, I had trained myself to ignore the incessant ping to recalculate while the foundation of my faith was eroding. College campuses filled with skeptics, critics, and intellectual bullies relish in their pursuit of muffling young Christians' spiritual navigation systems. Try as I might, the good news is that I couldn't completely silence it—no one can. So one evening, I found myself drawn to hear Josh McDowell speak.

Josh's faith journey began as a self-proclaimed agnostic—a person who believes that any ultimate reality (such as God) is unknown and probably unknowable.[55] Josh truly thought that Christianity was worthless.[56] Challenged to disprove Christianity, he labored in vain trying to defend his position. Ultimately, Josh concluded there was overwhelming evidence that Jesus Christ was indeed who He said He was—God. He shared his research in a book, *Evidence that Demands a Verdict*.

After plenty of wrong turns, I walked into the event unsure about my faith and who Jesus was to me—who He was to the world. As Josh thoughtfully answered the questions posed by attackers of the Christian faith—demystifying what the antagonists try to shroud in complexity and skepticism—the volume of the recalculating ping from my spiritual navigation system got cranked up.

The Power of the Cross

Reflecting on my experience with Josh McDowell and later with his son Sean, I realized reliable confidence (Godfidence) begins at the Cross.

> "God so loved the world that he gave his only
> Son, so that everyone who believes in him
> won't perish but will have eternal life."
> —John 3:16, NIV

"If we want proof of God's love for us, then we must look first at the Cross where God offered up His Son as a sacrifice for our sins. Calvary is the one objective, absolute, irrefutable proof of God's love for us."[57] Jesus said, "Come to me, all you who are weary and burdened, and I will give you rest" (Matthew 11:28, NIV). He's inviting us to set aside our *con*fidence, raise our eyes to the Cross, and embrace what He has done. Realizing what Jesus did on the Cross awakens our spiritual eyes. Regardless of how many wrong turns we take, how lost we become, or how fervently we try to silence His call to recalculate, He will continue to call us to Himself.

> **Realizing what Jesus did on the Cross awakens our spiritual eyes. Regardless of how many wrong turns we take, how lost we become, or how fervently we try to silence His call to recalculate, He will continue to call us to Himself.**

> "For the Son of Man has come to seek and to save the lost."
> —Luke 19:10, ESV

Like the little boy in chapter nine saying, "The Lord is my shepherd...This is all you need to know," I could stop here. This is all you need to know. Jesus' work on the cross is enough. Jesus is always enough. But throughout history, we've routinely rejected God's gift of redemptive grace. Even as He extends us the lifeline of grace that conquers doubt, discouragement, and disappointment, we turn Him away. We respond to seeing miracles as unexplained science and turn Him away. We experience miraculous victories in our lives and claim we secured them on our own and turn away from Him.

Turning away from God doesn't silence our spiritual navigation system because we are His own—created by Him for communion and relationship with Him. God never stops pursuing us. Even when we turn off course and go looking for confidence in all the wrong places or lose our confidence for all the wrong reasons, He still pursues us. We can count on God to persistently ping the spiritual navigation system of our souls with a reminder of the promise of the cross—recalculating.

> God never stops pursuing us. Even when we turn off course and go looking for confidence in all the wrong places or lose our confidence for all the wrong reasons, He still pursues us.

Absolutes in a Relativistic Culture

The United Nations invited a prominent Christian apologist to speak at their annual prayer breakfast. His ministry touching countries all over the world made him a friend of nations around the globe. He was assigned the topic, "The Search for Absolutes in a Relativistic Culture." He explained there were four areas we look for absolutes: evil, justice, love, and forgiveness. Then he began weaving them into a story. "You gather here [at the United Nations] to talk about evil empires. You look for just societies. What do you mean by that? You leave your loved ones back home, and you miss them—you know what love is about. Especially when you miss your loved ones so much—some of you are going to blow it and make mistakes, and you'll want to be forgiven."

The ambassadors were now on the edge of their seats. Riveted by the simplicity with which this intricate question was navigated, they leaned in. He then asked, "Where in the world do these four things converge in a single moment of human history?" He then repeated the question with inflection and intensity, "Where did evil, justice, love, and forgiveness converge at a moment in history?" He paused briefly to let them ruminate on the question. He was about to reveal a life-changing truth. He continued softly, invitingly, and slowly, "Can I take you to a hill called Calvary and show you the person of Jesus Christ? Who shows you the evil in your heart and mine—who was just and the justifier? Who loved us so greatly He gave Himself for us?"[58]

Our internal compass consistently directs us towards God. In 30 minutes, Ravi Zacharias infiltrated the spiritual navigation software of their souls—it was now pinging recalculating. Ravi's public legacy seemed secure when he died on May 19, 2020, at the age of 74. He spent his public life pointing people to Godfidence—preaching the cross's saving grace and providing answers for the faith believers have in Jesus. Millions of people were impacted and came to faith because of Ravi's work.

This manuscript had passed through its final proofing when the news broke of Ravi's gross personal misconduct. As I read through the shocking details of Ravi's effort to hide and advance his personal transgressions, I weighed the option (even necessity) of eliminating this story. Our cancel-oriented culture will cry out to bury Ravi's life's work. It's an option. But wiping Ravi's story from this book or removing his name from his namesake ministry doesn't change the absolute truth of God's love manifest in Jesus' work on the cross.

Ravi is a heartbreaking example of what happens if we live in *con*fidence. When we choose to ignore the ping to recalculate sounded by our spiritual software, Satan enters as "the thief [that] comes only to steal and kill and destroy" (John 10:10,

THE PROCESS RECALCULATING—FIX YOUR EYES ON JESUS

NIV). The enemy will use a single sin to cause us to stumble before we cross the finish line and destroy as many lives as he can along with it. The journey to the finish line—to finish strong—is an obstacle course filled with peril. It requires Godfidence that can only be found in Christ. The ping to recalculate directs us to His light. "The light shines in the darkness, and the darkness has not overcome it" (John 1:5, NIV).

A. W. Tozer said, "The Christian message rightly understood means this: The God who by the word of the Gospel proclaims men free, by the power of the Gospel actually makes them free. To accept less than this is to know the Gospel in word only, without its power."[59] If we ignore the pinging long enough, we are destined to fall into *con*fidence and dwell outside of the shelter of the Most High.[60] If we speak of the Gospel in word only, we will surely stumble on our way to the finish line. If we accept the power of the Gospel, we will never be too lost to find our way back to God.

> **If we speak of the Gospel in word only, we will surely stumble on our way to the finish line. If we accept the power of the Gospel, we will never be too lost to find our way back to God.**

Claim Your Godfidence

The bedrock of Godfidence is the cross—fix your eyes on Jesus. Unlike *con*fidence, Godfidence is reliable in all seasons and storms of life because it is powered by the One who died and rose again. The beauty of Godfidence is that it is a gift. All we have to do is claim it. In Christ, we become Godfident—connecting ourselves to the power of God.

> "For the word of the cross is foolishness to those who are perishing, but to us who are being saved it is the power of God."
> —1 Corinthians 1:18, NIV

Godfidence is the true north on our spiritual compass—reliably pointing us to Jesus and His redemptive work on the cross. Armed with Godfidence, we possess everything needed to navigate through every circumstance and condition of life—to finish strong.

> "Jesus was faithful over God's house as a Son.
> We are his house if we hold on to the confidence
> and the pride that our hope gives us."
> —Hebrews 3:6, CEB

CHAPTER 14
THE INVITATION—
WHAT DO WE DO WITH JESUS' INVITATION?

> "Listen! I am standing at the door and knocking! If anyone hears my voice and opens the door I will come into his home and share a meal with him, and he with me."
> —Revelation 3:20, NET

What if I turn down the invitation? I am sure you have been invited to attend an event and pondered the thought of turning it down. It gets more complicated when the request includes an RSVP that asks for "Regrets only," which means don't call or reply unless you are not coming. And if you don't call, we expect to see your smiling face. Argh, I hate that! My selfish little mind reacts with, "Why do I have to tell the host I am not coming?" Oh, I understand they are making plans. But I am sure they won't over-order on the iced tea I'd be drinking and I don't eat that much.

What are you going to do with Jesus' invitation? It is so easy to accept it in word but never ascend in our knowledge to surrender control of our lives and trust His loving dominion. God created us in His own image. He designed us to thrive, which can only be experienced by fully accepting Jesus' invitation.

> The stumbling block to Godfidence is that it is counterintuitive to our nature. It can't be secured without surrendering.

By default, the idea of surrendering control sparks a battle royal in our hearts and mind. Our fallen nature does not subscribe to waving white flags of surrender. Even when we feel overwhelmed and defeated, we reject the idea of submitting to any authority. We'd rather stubbornly push forward in our *con*fidence, despite knowing it can't save us. The stumbling block to Godfidence is that it is counterintuitive to our nature. It can't be secured without surrendering. Godfidence requires that we accept the invitation of God's gift of grace and reject the world.

Everyone's Invited

Jesus provides an incredible description of His invitation in the parable of the Great Banquet. He tells the Pharisees that a "certain man" (God) is preparing this festive banquet—the party that will define all parties. This is a once in a lifetime invitation—He's opening the doors to eternity. Jesus sends out messengers out asking for "Regrets only." He wants to make sure they know He is the one who is inviting them.

But the people just don't get it. Their regrets are a collection of lame excuses. In principle, they are insulting to the Master. But the Master does not give up. His love and kindness are so immense He pleads with the people. He holds nothing back trying to convince them this invitation is for real. He tells them, "Come, for everything is now ready." The iced tea is cold, the food is prepared, and the banquet hall is ready. Everything you could ever desire is here for you to taste and enjoy—come now, right now!

Jesus' invitation includes everyone—all-inclusive and without exception. He is offering them eternity (Godfidence) in exchange for their *con*fidence. It's a sure thing. He does not

THE INVITATION—WHAT DO WE DO WITH JESUS' INVITATION?

want you, me, or anyone to miss His invitation. Take a look at how the parable ends:

> "The servant said, 'Master, your instructions have been followed and there is still room.' The master said to the servant, 'Go to the highways and back alleys and urge people to come in so that my house will be filled. I tell you, not one of those who were invited will taste my dinner.'"
> —Luke 14:23-24, CEB

R.S.V.P., Please

Just think about what has taken place here? Everyone is invited—you, your neighbor, your friends, the family on the street corner, the outcasts, anyone and everyone. No exclusions, yet "there is still room." Can Jesus make His intent any clearer? He is on a mission to fill Heaven—it's an open invitation. Regrets only, but please don't concoct a lame excuse.

What's interesting is, Jesus does not tie a bow around the end of this parable—he leaves us with questions. We don't know if the people who rejected the invitation showed up. What we do know is this; Jesus' hand is extended. He wants us to join Him at the "Great Banquet." The invitation is permanent—that is, as long as the door is open.

What are you going to do with His invitation? When we accept His invitation, we grow in Godfidence because we get transformed by His grace, power, and strength. Godfidence emboldens us with courage.

> "God didn't give us a spirit that is timid but one that is powerful, loving, and self-controlled."
> —2 Timothy 1:7, CEB

"Recalculating." "Recalculating." I can't tell you how many times I've heard this alert ring in my ears. We may muffle it and learn to ignore it, but when we are off course, God will pursue us. "Go out to the roads and the country lanes and make them come in, so that my house will be full" (Luke 14:23b, NIV).

Look Who's Coming to Dinner

When I lose focus, I slip back into relying on *con*fidence. In mapping my course, pursuing my career, identifying my goals, and setting my priorities, I find myself on a collision course with God's will without realizing it. I can pray fervently for God to bless me and my plans. He answers these prayers by confronting me. Ultimately, He reminds me that, "For as the heavens are higher than the earth, so are [His] ways higher than [my] ways, and [His] thoughts than [my] thoughts" (Isaiah 55:9, ESV).

> God does not burst into our lives and take them over when we ignore His commands. We are volitional and ultimately the choice is ours.

I am learning on this journey that when you act in *con*fidence, you ignore God's invitation—choosing your own agenda. While this feels good at the moment, I can tell you from both experience and observation, it is not. God does not burst into our lives and take them over when we ignore His commands. We are volitional and ultimately the choice is ours. Jesus said,

> "Come to me, all you who are weary and burdened, and I will give you rest. Take my yoke upon you and learn from me, for I am gentle and humble in heart, and you will find rest for your souls. For my yoke is easy and my burden is light."
> —Matthew 11:28-30, NIV

Jesus' invitation is personal. He stands at the door of our lives and knocks. *Con*fidence distracts us from opening the door. It keeps us attentive to the false narratives of the world, created by man, in an attempt to fill the hole in our heart that which only Jesus can mend and heal.

I Regret to Inform You I Missed the Invitation

"Randy Pausch, the professor whose 'last lecture' made him a Lou-Gehrig-like symbol of the beauty and briefness of life, died [at the age of] 47."[61] As a book, *The Last Lecture* topped the bestseller lists and was translated into 30 languages. Jeff Zaslow, Pauch's co-author, said, "His fate is ours, sped up... He approached his illness as an optimist, a scientist, but also as a realist."[62]

"ABC News declared him one of its three 'Persons of the Year' for 2007. TIME magazine named him to its list of the 100 most influential people in the world. On thousands of Web sites, people wrote essays about what they had learned from him."[63] By every worldly measure, Dr. Pausch was successful. There was nothing shared that suggests he was not comfortable in his *con*fidence.

But in his last lecture, he failed to RSVP. Alistair Begg captures it perfectly, saying, "Randy Pausch, the 47-year old lecturer from Carnegie Mellon whose final lecture was an inspiration to everyone who heard it. And to those of us who heard snippets from it, who wouldn't be inspired by somebody who was able to speak so clearly to a generation he was about to leave behind concerning the importance of values, the importance of memories, the importance of family, and every other thing? Absolutely masterful all the way down the line with only one part missing."

> Confidence says, "I'm fine. Don't come to me with your invitation." Godfidence says I recognize I am carrying a heavy burden. I am weary and need you, Lord. Take my burden, Jesus. I hear your voice and accept your gift of grace.

The final paragraph reads, "Doctor Pausch gave practical advice in his lectures (now notice, here's the phrase) 'avoiding spiritual and religious matters.' He did however mention that he experienced a near-deathbed conversion: he switched and bought a Macintosh computer."[64] I suggest to you that that is a level of sardonic wit that can only be possessed by someone who has said, "Don't come to me with your invitation. I'm fine, thank you very much."[65]

*Con*fidence says, "I'm fine. Don't come to me with your invitation." Godfidence says I recognize I am carrying a heavy burden. I am weary and need you, Lord. Take my burden, Jesus. I hear your voice and accept your gift of grace. The good news is that Jesus continues to stand at the door and knock—as long as the invitation is open we can invite Him in.

"There are better things ahead than any we leave behind."[66]
—C. S. Lewis

CHAPTER 15
UNCOVERING YOUR PURPOSE
OUR IDENTITY IN CHRIST—
PURPOSEFUL AND POWERFUL

> "You may say to yourself, 'My power and the strength of my hands have produced this wealth for me.' But remember the Lord your God, for it is he who gives you the ability to produce wealth, and so confirms his covenant, which he swore to your ancestors, as it is today."
> —Deuteronomy 8:17-18, NIV

My youngest son, Andrew, is a self-described realist and a curious learner. I can always count on Andrew to search out the weakness in an argument and seek the moral high ground. So when he suggested I read *The Road to Character*, I was curious.

Battling for Character

The author, David Brooks, immediately captured my attention, writing, "Years pass and the deepest parts of yourself go unexplored and unstructured...You do not have a strategy to build character, and without that, not only your inner life but also your external life will eventually fall to pieces."[67] He described the "Road to Character" as an identity battle between Adam I and Adam II. Adam I wants "to have high status and win victories...and conquer the world." Adam II "wants to have a serene inner character, a quiet but solid sense of right and wrong—not only to do good but to be good...obey a calling...renounce worldly success and status."[68]

When I finished the book, I felt David was grappling with the enormity of the fact you only finish once (YOFO). I think he understood that *con*fidence would betray you on the way to the finish line. His words nibbled around the edges of the solution—Godfidence. He even described what it looks like, writing, "Occasionally, even today, you come across certain people who seem to possess an impressive inner cohesion. They are not leading fragmented, scattershot lives. They have achieved inner integration. They are calm, settled, and rooted. They are not blown off course by storms. They don't crumble in adversity. Their minds are consistent, and their hearts are dependable...They radiate a sort of moral joy. They answer softly when challenged harshly. They are silent when unfairly abused. They are dignified when others try to humiliate them, restrained when others try to provoke them...They are not thinking about what impressive work they are doing. They are not thinking about themselves at all. They just seem delighted by the flawed people around them. They just recognize what needs doing and they do it."[69]

The Road to Transformation

As I read this, I thought he could be describing the identity God appoints to us in Christ. Throughout the book, he inches his way to the foot of Calvary and stops. He was so close to pointing out that the bridge from Adam I to Adam II begins at the cross. Paul makes this clear in 1 Corinthians 15:22 (ESV), writing, "For as in Adam all die, so also in Christ all will be made alive." Paul is describing an essential truth about God's plan for dealing with humanity—there are only two men, Adam and Christ. We must choose who we want to be represented by before God. It can only be one or the other of these two men.

The road to transformation begins at the cross. This is the only place where Adam I will be able to recognize his *con*fidence is standing between him and who he wants to be—Adam II. The reality is Adam I is incapable of becoming Adam II without the atoning blood of Christ. **We must choose who we want to be represented by before God.** Adam II is a picture of Godfidence because recognizing his fragility, he understands that being created by God, he is subject to Him—totally dependent upon and accountable to Him.

> "For by him all things were created, in heaven and on earth, visible and invisible, whether thrones or dominions or rulers or authorities—all things were created through him and for him. And he is before all things, and in him all things hold together."
> —Colossians 1:16-17, ESV

We all think that we are smart enough not to fall into the trap of *con*fidence. "And no wonder, for Satan himself masquerades as an angel of light" (2 Corinthians 11:14, NIV). It's easy to read David Brooks' descriptions of Adam I and Adam II and intellectually understand the differences. But knowledge is not enough. Even Satan knows who Jesus is. And he demonstrated he knows God's Word better than most Christians, as shown in the wilderness when he tempted Jesus. Adam I stands *con*fidently at the foot of the Cross. There may be moments when he looks like a believer. But on the inside, he denies his need for a Savior. Adam II emerges into Godfidence by surrendering himself at the foot of the cross and being made alive in Christ.

Letting Go of Adam I

The pursuit of our identity in Christ is all about character. It is a real struggle. If we fail to understand "that the development of character is one of God's purposes for our lives, we will become frustrated by our circumstances."[70]

In the next section of this book, we will dig deeper into how to live in daily Godfidence. But before we close this chapter on the role of our identity in Christ as our link to transformation from *con*fidence to Godfidence, it's critical to acknowledge the reality of the struggle. If

> If we fail to understand "that the development of character is one of God's purposes for our lives, we will become frustrated by our circumstances."

you have stumbled and fallen, done the right things and experienced defeat, suffered under the weight of life's difficulties, and know Jesus without knowing His power in your life— I know how you feel. Living only in the knowledge of Christ and not in Christ leaves you in the grip of confidence and toiling in the desire to conquer the world on your own.

The road to Godfidence is not an event. I wish it were that easy. No quick fixes or "life hacks" to offer here. The enemy doesn't relinquish influence easily. It's a journey that begins when we've unmasked our *con*fidence, which gives us eyes to humbly acknowledge and accept the fact that our identity is in Christ.

> Living only in the knowledge of Christ and not in Christ leaves you in the grip of confidence and toiling in the desire to conquer the world on your own.

The words "in Christ" appear 272 times in the New Testament.[71] Paul uses the term 160 times[72] in his letters to express being united to Christ, each time reminding us that the only truly reliable source of power and strength in our lives is Christ, which is why Godfidence never fails. One place it appears is I Peter 5:10-11. Based on the notes in the margin of my Bible, I read this passage every day for over four months as I walked this road. In it, I discovered the beauty, simplicity, and strength of life in Christ revealed in 43 words.

> "And the God of all grace, who called you to his eternal glory in Christ, after you have suffered a little while, will himself restore you and make you strong, firm and steadfast. To him be the power for ever and ever. Amen."
> —1 Peter 5:10-11, NIV

Living Godfidently comes alive in Christ—to rest assured in the shelter of God's love and the grip of His grace. In Christ, we become a new creation—unleashing His power and strength in our lives, as well as accepting His dominion over us. These 43 words tell us that in Christ, our suffering will be temporary. In Christ, we will not suffer alone—He will return to us. In Christ, we will be made strong, firm, and steadfast. In Christ, we can praise Him with holy expectation. In Christ, His purpose for our lives will be fulfilled because He is the great "I Am." "To him be the power for ever and ever. Amen."[73]

> **Living Godfidently comes alive in Christ—to rest assured in the shelter of God's love and the grip of His grace.**

In Christ

Jesus is the solution to *con*fidence. In this life, we will always be imperfect and broken—it's inescapable. When we grow in the grace of who we are in Christ, we can stop trying to fix our imperfections and seek to elevate ourselves in the eyes of the world.

When Jesus becomes our central focus—our reason for existence—contentment replaces our anxiety, fears, and insecurities. We receive the gift of Godfidence when we start seeing ourselves as God sees us—created for a divine purpose that was ordained before we ever took a breath. In Christ, we are transformed into Godfident people—not in our strength, but in Christ's, He makes us unshakeable, immovable, resilient, and impermeable. God desires to use you. He does not see you the way you view yourself, especially on your worst days. Be sure, our creation-intended identity is revealed in our relationship with Christ.

CHAPTER 16
CLAIMING GOD'S PROMISES
A PROMISE IS A PROMISE—LEANING ON THE PROMISE MAKER

"If ever there is tomorrow when we're not together…
there is something you must always remember. You are
braver than you believe, stronger than you seem, and
smarter than you think. But the most important thing
is, even if we're apart…I'll always be with you."
—Christopher Robin, Winnie the Pooh

*Con*fidence won't always be with you—it's a fairy tale constructed by the enemy. He, like Christopher Robin, promises you the bravery, strength, and wisdom you'll need when it's required most. This is the *con*. It's all by enemy design. Use bold promises—tell you he will always be with you—to lure you in and pump you full of prideful self-reliance. Be sure, he is a

> Godfidence is where all good things come from because it is grounded in truth—God's absolute and irrevocable promises.

deceitful and unreliable promise maker. Godfidence is where all good things come from because it is grounded in truth—God's absolute and irrevocable promises.

The problem with living in the enemy-constructed fairy tale of *con*fidence is that it is deaf to the voice of truth. We are in danger of being swept deep into enemy territory when we can't hear the voice of truth telling us we are looking for our confidence in all the wrong places and losing our confidence for all the wrong reasons.

How to Claim a Promise

While God persistently pursues us with redemptive grace, our knowledge of Him—the great Creator, Provider, Sustainer, and Redeemer—is waning. Based on a 2019 Barna Research study that shaped the book *Good Faith*, the God of the Christian faith is growing less popular and relevant in today's culture. In the United States today, people are increasingly less likely to identify with and practice Christianity. And the younger you are, the more likely you are to recognize and embrace this trend.[74]

> Biblical literacy is essential to knowing God's promises. We can't claim his magnificent promises, rely on them to bolster our walk in every circumstance and condition of life, or share them as encouragement if we don't know them.

In this Barna study, they asked people about their Biblical curiosity. Using a scale of "strongly disagree" to "strongly agree," respondents were asked to consider the statement, "I am curious about what the Bible says." Nearly 35% of the respondents "somewhat or strongly disagreed" with the statement. While 37% "somewhat agreed," only 29% "strongly agreed."[75] What about you? Is it possible that a lack of Biblical literacy and curiosity is an obstacle to you living Godfidently?

Uncovering God's Promises

Biblical literacy is essential to knowing God's promises. We can't claim his magnificent promises, rely on them to bolster our walk in every circumstance and condition of life, or share them as encouragement if we don't know them.

Anne Graham Lotz beautifully explains the importance of craving Biblical literacy, writing, "Without Biblical literacy, you will never know God as He is, you will never know yourself as you are, you will never find and fulfill your reason for existence, you will never have authentic faith to sustain you or living hope to comfort you or unconditional love to compel you to follow Jesus. Without Biblical literacy, you are just guessing your way through life, and the chances are good that you are guessing wrong."[76]

A Promise is a Promise!

Godfidence stands upon God's promises. His Word is absolute truth, which makes Him a perfect and unfailing promise maker. So let's put God's promises as our solution to *con*fidence to a test. What do you think the probability is of one person, Jesus, fulfilling eight prophecies about the coming Messiah, written by different men, at various times and places, approximately 500 to 1,000 years before Jesus was born?

Dr. Peter Stoner explored this question in his book *Science Speaks*. Dr. Stoner, who served as the Chairman of the Mathematics Department at Pasadena City College and later the Chairman of the Science Division at Westmont College, calculated the probability using eight Old Testament prophecies.[77]

> Godfidence stands upon God's promises. His Word is absolute truth, which makes Him a perfect and unfailing promise maker.

1. The Messiah will be born in Bethlehem—Micah 5:2.

2. A messenger will prepare the way for the Messiah—Malachi 3:1.

3. The Messiah will enter Jerusalem as a king riding on a donkey—Zechariah 9:9.

4. The Messiah will be betrayed by a friend and suffer wounds in His hands—Zechariah 13:6.

5. The Messiah will be betrayed for 30 pieces of silver—Zechariah 11:12.

6. The betrayal money will be used to purchase a potter's field—Zechariah 11:13.

7. The Messiah will remain silent while He is afflicted—Isaiah 53:7.

8. The Messiah will die by having His hands and feet pierced—Psalm 22:16.

Dr. Stoner's peer-reviewed conclusion is mind-boggling.[78] "The chance that any man might have fulfilled all eight prophecies is one in 10 to the 17th power. That would be 1 in 100,000,000,000,000,000 (one hundred quadrillion)." To further illustrate the magnitude of Jesus fulfilling these prophecies, imagine laying 100,000,000,000,000,000 silver dollars over the geography of the state of Texas. Amongst the coins is a single silver dollar that has been painted red. Now you are blindfolded and told to find this red coin that lies in a two-foot deep blanket of coins covering all of Texas. Finding the coin is a measure of one man's probability of fulfilling eight unique prophecies, written by eight different prophets, over 500 years.[79]

> "Bible scholars tell us that nearly 300 references to 61 specific prophecies of the Messiah were fulfilled by Jesus Christ. The odds against one person fulfilling that many prophecies would be beyond all mathematical possibilities."

"Bible scholars tell us that nearly 300 references to 61 specific prophecies of the Messiah were fulfilled by Jesus Christ. The odds against one person fulfilling that many prophecies would be beyond all mathematical possibilities. It could never happen, no matter how much time was allotted. One mathematician's estimate of those impossible odds is 'one chance in a trillion, trillion, trillion, trillion, trillion, trillion, trillion, trillion, trillion, trillion, trillion, trillion, trillion.'"[80]

A PROMISE IS A PROMISE—LEANING ON THE PROMISE MAKER

God is a Reliable Promise Giver

Isaiah 40 is one of my favorite promises in Scripture. The opening verses inspired Handel's "Messiah." The closing verses found their way into the victorious story of Eric Liddell in the movie *Chariots of Fire*. Isaiah 40 beautifully describes God, the promise maker, and keeper—never failing and everlasting.

I carried a coin inscribed with the final three verses in my pocket for years.

> "Do you not know?
> Have you not heard?
> The Lord is the everlasting God,
>   the Creator of the ends of the earth.
> He will not grow tired or weary,
>   and his understanding no one can fathom.
> He gives strength to the weary
>   and increases the power of the weak.
> Even youths grow tired and weary,
>   and young men stumble and fall;
> but those who hope in the Lord
>   will renew their strength.
> They will soar on wings like eagles;
>   they will run and not grow weary,
>   they will walk and not be faint."
> —Isaiah 40: 28-31, NIV

Putting the coin in my pocket reminded me of God's promises—how He redeemed my dad's life. My dad left me the coin after he died. For many years, my dad trudged along with the heavy burden of pain and heartbreak etched upon his heart by the tragic losses of loved ones. I'll never forget the day he publicly surrendered His life to Jesus. I saw what the love and grace of Jesus can do—turning my steady and diligent dad into a loving and compassionate father. The promises in this passage anchored his Godfidence.

I remember when I reached into my pocket to discover the coin was not there—I lost it. I never found the coin. A piece of my dad disappeared with that coin. But the beauty of God's promises is that they are permanent and don't require a coin to claim them.

Claiming God's Promises

Without notice, life will present us with distractions, disappointments, and doubts that will blanket us in fog so thick we become disoriented and ultimately defeated. You might be in a fog right now. I understand what it feels like to struggle. When I looked back and was honest with myself, I felt sorry for myself. In my prideful mind, it was justified. I lost my dreams. I lost my income and health insurance. I lost people who I thought would be friends for life. I lost sight of God, but He kept his eyes on me. We may fall (we will fall), but a promise is a promise—Jesus said, "I will never leave you nor forsake you" (Hebrews 13:5).

> "God's care for his children is like the sun: it's constant. Even though the clouds obscure it, it doesn't mean the sun isn't there."

Claiming God's promises became the seeds that allowed Godfidence to blossom into hope and a new vision. Alistair Begg paints a beautiful word picture of this, writing, "God's care for his children is like the sun: it's constant. Even though the clouds obscure it, it doesn't mean the sun isn't there."[81] God's promises always shine as bright as the sun. A promise is a promise—"write them on the tablet of your heart" (Proverbs 7:3, NIV).

CHAPTER 17
DRESS THE PART—
PUTTING ON THE FULL ARMOR OF GOD

> "Faith today is treated as something that only should make us different, not that actually does or can make us different. In reality we vainly struggle against the evils of this world, waiting to die and go to heaven. Somehow we've gotten the idea that the essence of faith is entirely a mental and inward thing."
> —Dallas Willard

I picked up *The Hole in the Gospel* while on vacation in the summer of 2009. I've referred to this book many times over the past few years as I've thought about Godfidence and what is necessary to finish strong. In the book's introduction, Richard Stearns poses a question, "What does God expect of me?" His answer grabbed my full attention, "A Christian, or follower of Jesus Christ requires much more than just have a personal transforming relationship with God. It also entails a public and transforming relationship with the world."[82]

"What does God expect of me?"

Reframing his answer as a question confronts us with a bold challenge, "As a follower of Jesus Christ, are you engaged in developing a public and transforming relationship with the world?" This is not a rhetorical question. The essence of our faith is not a mental exercise in self-reflection. "God didn't give us a spirit that is timid but one that is powerful, loving, and self-controlled" (2 Timothy 1:7). The grip of *con*fidence blankets us in timidity. It inhibits us from developing a transforming relationship with God that prepares us to accept His divinely appointed purpose for our lives.

> "As a follower of Jesus Christ, are you engaged in developing a public and transforming relationship with the world?"

We rarely think we are ready to engage when God calls us because it will pull us away from who we think we are in the world. For Richard Stearns, it meant resigning as the CEO of Lenox and becoming the President of World Vision—a global Christian humanitarian organization. Stearns said, "I was convinced they had the wrong person. I had never been to Africa. I knew very little about global poverty. I had no theological training, and I'd never done much public speaking. I was running a luxury goods company, of all things—selling expensive baubles to the wealthy."[83]

> **The grip of confidence blankets us in timidity.**

Better Than Armor

*Con*fidence is inherently hesitant because it doesn't resolve our doubts. It only keeps outsiders from seeing we are prideful, shaking, and weak on the inside. When presented with God-centric opportunities, my *con*fident response was, "Let me pray about it." This gave time for my unreliable feelings to rise up and conclude, "It just doesn't feel right." As a result, I'd decline the assignment and slip back into the comfort of my *con*fident worldly identity—looking Christian on the outside and struggling with surrendering to Christ on the inside.

If we are going to live out our faith in the world and accept mission-critical assignments, we need Godfidence, which requires putting on the full armor of Christ. I have a friend whose love for the Lord spills out onto everyone he meets and into every aspect of his life. I've learned a lot about Godfidence from Bill. He loves talking about putting on the armor of God that Paul describes in Ephesians 6:13-17, NIV:

> Confidence is inherently hesitant because it doesn't resolve our doubts. It only keeps outsiders from seeing we are prideful, shaking, and weak on the inside.

"Therefore, <u>put on every piece of God's armor</u> so you will be able to resist the enemy in the time of evil. Then after the battle you will still be standing firm. Stand your ground, putting on the <u>belt of truth</u> and the <u>body armor of God's righteousness</u>. <u>For shoes, put on the peace</u> that comes from the Good News so that you will be fully prepared. In addition to all of these, hold up the <u>shield of faith</u> to stop the fiery arrows of the devil. <u>Put on salvation as your helmet</u>, and take the <u>sword of the Spirit</u>, which is the word of God. Pray in the Spirit at all times and on every occasion. Stay alert and be persistent in your prayers for all believers everywhere."

I remember Bill describing putting on the belt, shoes, shield, helmet, and sword in God's armor and what each means [underlined above—my emphasis]. Then he asked, "Do you know the only place on your body that is unprotected by God's armor?" I told him I'd never considered this question. I was stumped, but very curious to know the answer. Do you know? Bill said, "There is no armor on your back. God gives you something better than armor. He places his hand on your back to protect and guide you."

Putting on God's Armor

When we "put on every piece of God's armor," we intentionally exchange the unreliability of *confidence* for the armor of

Godfidence. This gives us the assurance after the battle that we will still be standing firm. Jesus knew this journey to follow Him and make Him known in the world would be tough. Praying for his disciples, Jesus lifts this petition to God, "My prayer is not that you take them out of the world but that you protect them from the evil one. They are not of the world, even as I am not of it. Sanctify them by the truth; your word is truth" (John 17:15-17).

> Dressing in the armor of God enables us to accept our weaknesses, depend less on our talent and resources, and more on God's desire to work in and through us.

Godfidence enables us to focus our attention on what God is calling us to do—opening us up to His equipping. God wastes nothing. He uses every experience and outcome, both good and bad, to equip us for His call. Dressing in the armor of God enables us to accept our weaknesses, depend less on our talent and resources, and more on God's desire to work in and through us.

Prepare My Heart to Respond

In August 2018, I received an unexpected phone call inquiring if I would be interested in exploring a role with CRISTA Ministries as their CEO. After a couple of exploratory phone calls, I couldn't help but think, "Oh, this is what you were preparing me for, Lord." The position checked all my boxes for a call. It provided a foundation for significant Kingdom impact. The structure and focus of the ministry aligned with my experience and gifts. And it appeared the people I'd be working with were incredible.

As the process evolved, my wife and I earnestly prayed for direction. I met with Ed Ewart, my pastor, who put everything in perspective, "Let the process unfold, Jim. Take a front-row seat to watch God at work," he said. Pastor Ed's comments made me think of *The Hole in the Gospel*. I began imagining God doing the same thing with me that he did with Richard Stearns.

Eventually, they asked me to meet with Price Harding from CarterBaldwin. Price was heading up the candidate search for CRISTA. I liked Price immediately. After our meeting, I was *con*fident I was watching God unveil my next assignment. A few days later, my primary contact, Chris Hornsby, called to tell me CRISTA was going to pursue another candidate.

C. S. Lewis said, "Our highest activity must be response, not initiative."[84] I felt deep in my heart that God had been preparing me over the prior five years for this call. I responded. Richard Stearns responded. Our highest activity is to respond when God stirs in our hearts to move. What we see happening and what God does will not, maybe even rarely, turn out the way we expect or envision. We may be surprised, elated or even disappointed at the moment. But we will eventually see it turned out perfectly—His glory, not ours. By dressing the part—putting on our armor, we can Godfidently take a front-row seat and say, "Yes, Lord," and watch God at work.

> Our highest activity is to respond when God stirs in our hearts to move. What we see happening and what God does will not, maybe even rarely, turn out the way we expect or envision.

PART FOUR
LIVING IN DAILY GODFIDENCE

"Life is a place for proving whose strength you trust—man's or God's. Life is not a place for proving the power of your intelligence to know truth. It's a place for proving the power of God's grace to show truth."
—John Piper

"Knowledge is power."[85] Sir Francis Bacon made this statement in 1597. He was the world's last human know-it-all. Today, smartphone technology has made everyone a know-it-all. Cheap and ready access to information has not only commoditized knowledge; it falsely dresses it up as wisdom. Ready access to information has not made us abundantly wiser. Alistair Begg sums up our condition beautifully, saying, "In our quest for knowledge, we find ourselves wandering in a wasteland of our own ingenuity because our knowledge is devoid of truth."[86]

> Cheap and ready access to information has not only commoditized knowledge; it falsely dresses it up as wisdom. Ready access to information has not made us abundantly wiser.

Wisdom does not come with a college degree. Even life experience does not guarantee we will become wise. Solomon learned throughout his life that godly wisdom is not secured through the acquisition of worldly knowledge but the earnest pursuit of knowing God and the desire for a relationship with Him. To this end, Solomon reveals the mind of God in the book of Proverbs. This treasure of wisdom is built upon one verse.

> **Knowledge devoid of objective truth is incapable of producing the spiritual and moral wisdom required to address life's essential questions and problems.**

"The fear of the Lord is the beginning of knowledge; but fools despise wisdom and instruction."
—Proverbs 1:7, NIV

Knowledge devoid of objective truth is incapable of producing the spiritual and moral wisdom required to address life's essential questions and problems. God is the exclusive source of the wisdom and truth needed to finish strong.

Knowledge Can Never Be Enough

I was a fool. With my eyes set on the world, I refused any guidance that suggested I was heading for a crash. Dripping with confidence, I was blind to the arrogant pride that fueled my willful defiance of wisdom and instruction. This taught me a painful lesson—if you allow other fools to set your standards and shape your dreams, you'll never gain the wisdom that comes from rightly acting on God's truth. Paul makes this clear to us, writing, "For the foolishness of God is wiser than human wisdom, and the weakness of God is stronger than human strength" (1 Corinthians 1:25, NIV).

> **If you allow other fools to set your standards and shape your dreams, you'll never gain the wisdom that comes from rightly acting on God's truth.**

Knowing the facts will never be enough. Knowledge of the cross is not enough. Awareness of Christ's invitation is not enough. Learning about the strength of your identity in Christ is not enough. The knowledge of God's promises is not enough. I knew all of these things. You either knew or now know them too. But it didn't make me wise to the fact *con*fidence had groomed me to be irreverent, indifferent at best, to who God truly is—the Creator, Preserver, and Redeemer of the world.

Beginning with God All Over Again

Earnestly seeking God with my whole heart is where this journey to Godfidence began. Early in this process, A. W. Tozer's book, *God's Pursuit of Man*, helped me understand how I got stuck in *con*fidence. He wrote, "It cannot but be a major tragedy in life of any man to live in a church from childhood to old age and know nothing more real than some synthetic god compounded of theology and logic, but having no eyes to see, no ears to hear and no heart to love."[87]

I saw myself in Tozer's description—*con*fidence guiding my life into "a major tragedy...no eyes to see, no ears to hear and no heart to love." If you are not experiencing the power of the living God in your life, you, too, must see yourself in Tozer's description. You know deep within your soul, something is missing. Apart from God, a desperate yearning perpetually churns within you because you were created with an internal compass that points you to Jesus—you were created by God and for God.

> Apart from God, a desperate yearning perpetually churns within you because you were created with an internal compass that points you to Jesus—you were created by God and for God.

History reveals that those who knew God best made study and prayer time a priority. Tozer reinforces this, writing, "The man who would know God must give time to Him. He must count no time wasted which is spent in cultivation of His acquaintance. He must give himself to meditation and prayer hours on end."[88]

Building Blocks of Godfidence

As tough as it is to admit, my pride stood in the way of making God a priority—let alone my principal aim in life. As God confronted me with my pride, He taught me the importance of giving Him time. In these moments of silence, study, prayer, and reflection, He shaped my thinking about Godfidence.

The 12th chapter of Romans was very instructive. For the better part of a year, I read the opening verses, day after day, for weeks. In the first four verses, Paul describes what is required to act on our knowledge of Christ's gift of salvation. He pleads with us to do four things. These are the cornerstones for letting go of our *con*fidence and experiencing the Godfidence that grows out of an intimate relationship with the living God.

Cornerstone #1: Surrender to God. (12:1, AMP)

> "Therefore I urge you, brothers and sisters, by the mercies of God, to present your bodies [dedicating all of yourselves, set apart] as a living sacrifice, holy and well-pleasing to God, which is your rational (logical, intelligent) act of worship."

When I see the word "therefore," in Scripture, I've learned to pay close attention. "Therefore" is an imperative—linking a statement of fact to a command or instruction for living. Paul uses "therefore," in this case, to tell us how we should respond to our knowledge of Jesus, His redemptive work on the cross, His invitation of grace, and His promises.

In Chapter One, I asked, "Are you a gambler—willing to bet your life on the belief that self-confidence is not a *con*?" Paul is telling us it is a losing proposition. He reinforces the fact that we have ample proof to put our full faith and trust in Jesus. Therefore, it's time to move from indifference to all in; from involved to committed so that we can become Godfident.

Cornerstone #2: Separate yourself from (*con*fidence) the world. (12:2 AMP)

"And do not be conformed to this world [any longer with its superficial values and customs], but be transformed and progressively changed [as you mature spiritually] by the renewing of your mind [focusing on godly values and ethical attitudes], so that you may prove [for yourselves] what the will of God is, that which is good and acceptable and perfect [in His plan and purpose for you]."

*Con*fidence is a magnet that draws you into the world. Its nature conforms you to the world because *con*fidence is built upon superficial values and pop culture. Being transformed into Godfidence is not an event. Spiritual maturity is a journey that changes your attitude towards the world, aligns your heart with godly values, and prepares you to receive His purpose for your life.

> Being transformed into Godfidence is not an event. Spiritual maturity is a journey that changes your attitude towards the world, aligns your heart with godly values, and prepares you to receive His purpose for your life.

Cornerstone #3: Set your pride aside—quench the fuel of *con*fidence. (12:3, AMP)

"For by the grace [of God] given to me I say to everyone of you not to think more highly of himself [and of his importance and ability] than he ought to think; but to think so as to have sound judgment, as God has apportioned to each a degree of faith [and a purpose designed for service]."

For the first 53 years of my life, I never prayed for God to reveal my pride. Day after day, returning to this verse confronted me with the necessity of asking God to expose my pride, seek His grace, and allow Him to set my course.

The journey to Godfidence is much like that of a strong and skilled riverboat pilot. Your charge is to not think too highly of yourself, but to study the river each and every day, all over again, because it changes daily. An open channel one day may become a sand bar that could gut your boat the next. Only a humble student of the river with an eye to changing circumstances and conditions makes it through. Godfidence does not assure you will know it all. Instead, it gives rise to a humble and teachable spirit that relies upon God to get you through.

> **Godfidence does not assure you will know it all. Instead, it gives rise to a humble and teachable spirit that relies upon God to get you through.**

Cornerstone #4: Trust you are in good hands. (12:11-12, AMP)

"Never lagging behind in diligence; aglow in the Spirit, enthusiastically serving the Lord; constantly rejoicing in hope [because of our confidence in Christ], steadfast and patient in distress, devoted to prayer [continually seeking wisdom, guidance, and strength]."

Godfidence is reliable because it is anchored in the truth of God's grace. God loves you, God is with you, God is for you, and God will never fail you. In Christ, you can trust that you are in good hands.

Living in Daily Godfidence

You might be familiar with the adage, "It's not how you start that matters, but how you finish." Living in daily Godfidence is the key to finishing well—finishing strong. In Part Four, we'll build on the foundation we've just laid by adding five Godfidence building strategies.

- Truth, Faith, & Prayer—Holy Anticipation and Expectation
- Take Every Thought Captive

- Put First Things First
- Build a Deep-Water Faith
- Keep Your Eyes on the Finish Line

> "It is better to trust in the Lord than
> to put confidence in man."
> —Psalm 118:8, NIV

CHAPTER 18
TRUTH, FAITH, PRAYER—HOLY ANTICIPATION AND EXPECTATION

"The possibilities of prayer run parallel
with the promises of God."
—E. M. Bounds

There was something wrong. Scott knew it. It was obvious. All you had to do was look at him. But doctors couldn't explain why Scott had stopped growing. The search for answers meant Scott's life revolved around doctor visits and hospital stays. Only by accident, he found himself standing on the ice at the skating club near his home.

A few short years later, Scott Hamilton was the face of men's figure skating in the world. From 1980 to 1984, Scott would accomplish something that has never been matched—he won 16 consecutive national and world championships and Olympic gold.

In 1997, at the height of his professional skating career, Scott was diagnosed with testicular cancer. The ensuing chemotherapy treatments put Scott's career on hold. It burdened him with memories of his mom's unsuccessful fight with cancer. As Scott struggled with his fear, his future wife, Tracie, introduced him to Pastor Ken Durham.

A Turning Point

Ken said something that resonated with Scott, "You have to understand that Christianity is a faith of history. These things actually happened."[89] Scott describes this as a turning point in his life, saying, "I understand that through a strong relationship with Jesus you can endure anything...God is there to guide you through the tough spots. God was there every single time, every single time."[90]

> "You have to understand that Christianity is a faith of history. These things actually happened."

Scott and Tracie got married in 2002. They prayed Scott's cancer treatment would not preclude them from starting a family. Nine months and two days later, Aidan was born. Having been adopted himself, Scott said it was the first time he'd ever looked into eyes that looked just like his and seen flesh of his flesh. Scott, believing his health problems were behind him, was shocked to be told he had a brain tumor five months later. In the moments after he told Tracie, she took his hands and started to pray. "It was in that moment, I knew where I was going to put everything."[91] The biopsy revealed Scott was born with the tumor. It was the reason he stopped growing as a kid. God had a plan. This tumor that kept Scott from growing was also the reason why he became a skater.

After the complete removal of the tumor, it returned six years later. This time Scott said, "I didn't see past it this time. I didn't think I'd survive."[92] Scott was feeling overwhelmed, weak, and uncomfortable. While awake in the hospital at 3 a.m., one of the nurses asked Scott if she could get him anything. The conversation that ensued changed the way Scott looked at prayer and God forever.

Scott replied to her offer, "No, I'm just a little scared." "Do you pray?" she asked. "Yes, I do," Scott replied. Taking his lead she asked, "What do you say when you pray?" "Well," Scott replied, "I just thank God for all the blessings in my life." The nurse took Scott deeper, "Do you ever ask Him for anything?" "No, I just want Him to know I'm grateful," Scott replied—demonstrating his humility and exposing his fear. The nurse pressed Scott for more, "Who is God to you?" Scott paused for a moment and offered, "Well, I guess He's my Father." "Oh," she said, nodding acknowledgment, "You're a father, right?" Scott nodded yes. Her next question changed Scott's view of prayer forever. "If one of your children was hurting wouldn't you want him to come to you for comfort and strength?" Now softly weeping, Scott nodded and said, "Yes."[93]

> It's foreign to most of us to pray with expectant anticipation based on the God of all creation is interested in hearing about what stirs within our hearts. It begs the question, "Who is God to you?"

Who is God to You?

I'm drawn to Scott Hamilton's spiritual transparency. I think he saw God the way most of us see Him—worthy of our praise, deserving of our gratitude, but above our requests. It's foreign to most of us to pray with expectant anticipation based on the God of all creation is interested in hearing about what stirs within our hearts. It begs the question, "Who is God to you?"

Your answer to this question says everything about your view and use of prayer. We must remember that "through Christ, more specifically through our union with Christ, we have continual and confident access to God, whom we may freely and rightly address as Father."[94] E. M. Bounds describes what Godfident prayer looks like, writing, "The secret of success in Christ's Kingdom is the ability to pray."[95] Praying expectantly honors God because it acknowledges who He is—the Creator,

> "The secret of success in Christ's Kingdom is the ability to pray." Praying expectantly honors God because it acknowledges who He is—the Creator, Owner, and Authority over all things.

TRUTH, FAITH, PRAYER—HOLY ANTICIPATION AND EXPECTATION

Owner, and Authority over all things. "In the morning, Lord, you hear my voice; in the morning I lay my requests before you and wait expectantly" (Psalm 5:3, NIV).

Ask

If you were one of the disciples, what would you have asked of Jesus? Their unique relationship with Jesus positioned them to ask for anything—instructions on sharing the Gospel, healing people, performing miracles, or maybe studying the Scriptures. But they didn't ask for any of these things. Instead, they asked Jesus for the one thing they needed to fulfill the assignment He would soon give them. They asked Him to teach them to pray.

> "It happened that while Jesus was praying in a certain place, after He finished, one of His disciples said to Him, 'Lord, teach us to pray just as John also taught his disciples.'"
> —Luke 11:1, AMP

Jesus repeatedly demonstrated prayer was the source of His strength. Everything Jesus did was preceded by prayer. Jesus taught the disciples how to pray using what we know as the Lord's Prayer. He beautifully weaves together six all-encompassing requests in this prayer. I think Jesus wanted to impress upon them that they were fully dependent upon their Heavenly Father for everything. If the disciples were going to live in faith and carry the message of Christ's redemptive grace into the world, it was impossible without bringing their requests to God.

Prayer honors God, acknowledges our dependence upon His grace, and gives rise to Godfidence.

The necessity Jesus placed on prayer reveals He was fully human—totally vulnerable and expressly dependent upon the Father for the strength to complete His purpose. Honest prayer is vulnerable. Prayer honors God, acknowledges our dependence upon His grace, and gives rise to Godfidence. "With God's power working in us, God can do much, much more than anything we can ask or imagine."[96]

Praying Honestly

Before I embarked upon this spiritual journey to Godfidence, I treated prayer casually—like something a "good Christian" was supposed to do. I'd pray at the dinner table because it was an excellent example to set for my family. Still, beyond that, it wasn't a priority. It pains me to consider that my boys could think I prayed out of obligation rather than as an offering of gratitude and love.

Reflecting on my *con*fident prayers, I can assure you they were shallow and self-righteous. When God heard my voice, He had to be disappointed I did little more than try to impress Him and offer up a shopping list of what I wanted Him to do for me. When you believe you are in control—*con*fident—how else would you pray? The problem with prayer rising from *con*fidence is that it keeps God from giving us what we need most and what He most wants to give us—Himself.

The problem with prayer rising from confidence is that it keeps God from giving us what we need most and what He most wants to give us—Himself.

After getting fired, I desperately tried to revive my *con*fidence and resisted the fact that I needed to change. Cracking through the pride that *con*fidence wrapped me in was tough. In the grip of *con*fidence, you don't realize you've made company with a deceitful and fruitless companion. As God peeled back the layers of my *con*fidence, He allowed me to see who I truly am—who we all are—weak, vulnerable, and dependent upon Him.

Confidence crowds God out and is opposed to the stillness honest prayer requires.

Candidly, I didn't know how to pray—evidence of me trying to impress God with my prayers. Go ahead and chuckle. The audacity to think I could impress Him is funny. God did want to hear the desires of my heart, but not a laundry list of how He could serve my needs. I am absolutely sure of this; if you show up to pray with a heart and mind full of yourself, there is no room for God. *Con*fidence

TRUTH, FAITH, PRAYER—HOLY ANTICIPATION AND EXPECTATION

crowds God out and is opposed to the stillness honest prayer requires.

So, I just started showing up. I found Psalm 46:10, "Be still, and know that I am God,"[97] to be instructive and helpful. I would sit down, close my eyes, and repeat slowly, "Be still and know that I am God," over and over—pausing from time to time to just be still. This was the gateway for me becoming less and God becoming more. Stillness precedes knowing God and gives Godfidence room to grow.

> **Stillness precedes knowing God and gives Godfidence room to grow.**

Godfidence—Praying with Holy Anticipation and Expectation

> "So we can go confidently to the throne of God's kindness to receive mercy and find kindness, which will help us at the right time."
> —Hebrews 4:16, GWT

Giving ourselves over to the gift of God's grace lifts the weight of sin that confines us in *con*fidence. "Grace with confidence" is Godfidence—access to the Father through prayer based on Jesus's work on the cross.

Godfident prayers are:

- <u>Bold</u>. Rising out of holy anticipation and expectation of His provision, bold prayers honor and glorify God. "To request things of God, not that our selfish desires might be satisfied but that his name might be glorified."[98]

- <u>Frequent</u>. "It's important that you keep asking God to show you what He wants you to do. If you don't ask, you won't know."[99]

- <u>Specific</u>. Specific prayers are honest, authentic, and revealing. They help cultivate our relationship with

God, understand our desires and see His hand move from our prayers. When I pray specifically, it's clear to me when He has answered my prayers. This strengthens my faith and gives me the Godfidence to ask him to do even more.

- <u>Persistent</u>. "The secret of prayer and its success lies in its urgency. We must press our prayers upon God."[100]

- <u>Honoring</u>. Jesus says, "If you remain in me and follow my teachings, you can ask anything you want, and it will be given to you" (John 15:7, NCV). This is one of the richest promises in all of Scripture. "The conclusion, then, is this: if you are abiding in him, and his words are abiding in you and you want to serve him and bear his fruit, then you can take this to the bank, you truly can ask for anything and it will be done for you! This is based on the authority of the infallible words of Jesus himself."[101]

Let me reemphasize my journey to Godfidence was paved by and continues to be molded by the wise counsel of many outstanding Bible teachers. Craig Hazen was incredibly helpful in this area of prayer. Dr. Hazen, speaking about John 15:7, wrote, "We often find this promise difficult because we are immersed in a culture that simply does not think supernatural things (like answers to prayer) happen." He's pinpointing the problem with *con*fidence. He went on to say, "This affects us all—no matter how spiritual we are. But the Lord can help us overcome it."[102] It's Jesus that paves the pathway from *con*fidence to Godfidence.

Godfidence rises when we pray with holy anticipation and expectation. "[Don't] let those who might abuse this passage (John 15:7) rob [you] of gleaning the wonderful promise that the Lord himself had in store for us."[103] Ask—pray with holy anticipation and expectation.

CHAPTER 19
TAKE EVERY THOUGHT CAPTIVE

"The mind feasts on what it focuses on. What consumes my thinking will be the making or the breaking of my identity."
—Lysa TerKeurst

Can you imagine stepping into your office every day knowing a single mistake could cost you your life and the lives of people you love? Naval aviators live in this world. There is no room for mistakes. In the cockpit of a fighter jet, the rules of engagement are written in blood. These men and women are Top Gun aviators—modern-day gladiators.

Jim DiMatteo, retired US Navy Captain, is the most decorated Naval aviator in history—a Top Gun legend. Captain DiMatteo, describing the makeup of a Top Gun fighter pilot's confidence, says, "It's 50% character, 25% preparation, and 24% experience and learning." These are the ingredients that make up 99% of the recipe that gets a fighter pilot to the boarding ladder of their aircraft. It's the remaining 1% that glues the recipe altogether and assures a successful mission. "The last 1%," DiMatteo says, "is your inner dialogue. It's what you say to yourself at the precise moment you are called on to perform."[104]

It's critical—if a Top Gun pilot's thinking is not right, they can talk themselves out of the 99% that is required to succeed.

Jet fighter pilots are confident but not arrogant. There is no room for ego or artistic interpretation when lives are on the line and you've been entrusted with flying a multi-million dollar aircraft. The rules of engagement are "written in blood" because they were deconstructed from deadly missions. Every rule defines reality—life and death decision-making. Every pilot follows them without exception. Yet, fatal mistakes are made—why? The underlying cause of 80% to 90% of fighter pilot fatalities is traceable to mental distraction. Something bothering them away from work that interfered with their inner dialogue—they lost their glue. At a mission-critical moment when 100% mental focus and presence were required, their minds wandered.

> Our enemy doesn't intend to engage us in physical combat. His strategy is to defeat us before we accept our purposeful mission by stealing our glue—distracting our inner dialogue and focus.

Do you know what you share in common with a Top Gun Naval aviator? Every day you too are engaged in deadly combat. Our enemy doesn't intend to engage us in physical combat. His strategy is to defeat us before we accept our purposeful mission by stealing our glue—distracting our inner dialogue and focus. By winning the battle for our thoughts, the enemy mentally defeats us—assuring we never step into the arenas God calls us to. Our rules of engagement are written with Christ's blood—they hold the key to living Godfidently and aren't open to individual interpretation.

The Battle is Mental

You must take every thought captive to live Godfidently. Paul spells the fight out in 2 Corinthians 10:3-5, CEB:

> "Although we live in the world, we don't fight our battles with human methods. Our weapons that we fight with aren't human, but instead they are powered

by God for the destruction of fortresses. They destroy arguments, and every defense that is raised up to oppose the knowledge of God. They capture every thought to make it obedient to Christ. Once your obedience is complete, we are ready to punish any disobedience."

We talk to ourselves at a rate of 4,000 words per minute—a dizzying ten to twenty times faster than our speaking voice.[105] Our mind processes 50,000 to 80,000 thoughts a day, 80% of them being the same thoughts we had yesterday, and 98% of those thoughts are negative.[106] The character of our inner dialogue is a loop of repetitively negative chatter. How can this be? Dr. Rick Hanson, a neuropsychologist, says, "We possess an ancient brain operating in a modern world. In effect, the brain is like Velcro for negative experiences, but Teflon for positive ones."[107]

To plug into Godfidence, you must take every thought captive. In *con*fidence, the enemy overwhelms our minds and hijacks our thinking. Consider the impact of consuming five-minutes of negative news a day for 30 days. Dr. Jack Haskins, a professor at the University of Tennessee, proved it dramatically alters our thinking and inner dialogue.

Selecting participants who were predisposed to optimism, Dr. Haskins had them listen to five minutes of negative news a day for 30 days. At the end of the study, they were more depressed than before, began to believe the negative things they heard would soon happen to them, were less inclined to help others in need, and thought the world was a more negative place than before.[108] All it took to inflict significant mental damage was five minutes of negative news a day.

The Fight is Real

The spiritual battlefield is intense. A quick look at our interaction with smartphones, engagement with social media, and the use of the Internet demonstrates that our effort to take every thought captive faces resistance.

- Adults spend between 3.5 and 4.5 hours a day on their mobile devices.[109]
- Teens spend 7 hours and 22 minutes a day on their mobile devices.[110]
- We check our phones an average of 58 times a day.[111]
- You are 63% more likely to click on a negative headline.[112]
- Negative news holds a 17 to 1 advantage over positive news.
- One-third of people interact on social media more than ten times per day.[113]
- Multiple studies strongly link heavy social media use and an increased risk for depression, anxiety, loneliness, self-harm, and suicidal thoughts.[114]
- The average teenager views ten hours of media a day.[115]
- We conduct an average of 1,200 web searches a month.[116]

As daunting as these facts are, they provide only a small snippet of the emerging battlefield. The exploding consumption of online pornography is an emerging cultural tsunami that is disarming us—fully capable of destroying us.

- Fifty-one percent of men and sixteen percent of women at North American universities spend up to five hours a week online for sexual purposes and another 11% of men spend from five to 20 hours a week.[117]
- Various international studies target porn consumption rates at 50 percent to 99 percent among men, and 30 percent to 86 percent among women.[118]

- A 2016 research study conducted by Barna Group found that:
  - "Porn use is fueled by a new moral code embraced by society that says (1) people should not criticize someone else's life choices, (2) people can believe whatever they want as long as their beliefs don't impact society, and (3) any kind of sexual expression between two consenting adults is acceptable."
  - "A new type of pornography has emerged. Porn 2.0—often self-created, shared with friends or significant others, includes sexting and is encouraged and rewarded by celebrities like Kim Kardashian. Porn 2.0 offers the same trauma and harms as traditional porn."[119]
- During the COVID-19 pandemic, Pornhub offered free access to its content, resulting in traffic to the site rising 24%.[120]

Understand that whatever you focus on changes your thinking. We are interacting with the enemy's tools every day. This persistent interaction with our mobile devices and the Internet allows the enemy to infiltrate our minds and turn holy anticipation into anxiety. It stifles holy expectation and replaces it with doubt and fear.

Mission Critical Thinking

Mental battle lines are drawn around strongholds—thought fortresses designed to move you towards Godfidence (the character of God) or *con*fidence (the lies of the enemy).

God's Strongholds	Satan's Strongholds
• Hope	• Worry
• Faith	• Doubt and anxiety
• Holy expectations	• Worldly expectations
• God's promises	• Self-reliance
• Community	• Isolation
• Gratitude	• Envy and comparison
• Stillness	• Busyness
• Peace	• Fear
• Abundance	• Scarcity
• Give	• Get
• Claim Jesus as Lord	• Embrace the world
• Humility	• Pride
• Marriage—sexual purity	• Sexual immorality

You are flying a distracted mission when your attention drifts into enemy territory. Peril awaits anyone who does not respect Satan's schemes. Be sure he doesn't have to strike a decisive blow. Distracted thinking, even briefly, is all it takes for him to weaken your reasoning, impair your conscience, obscure your vision and compromise God's authority in your life.

Strategies for Taking Every Thought Captive

> "God gave us a spirit not of fear but of power and love and self-control."
> —2 Timothy 1:7, ESV

Here are some battle equipping strategies you can employ today to plug into Godfidence. Each is framed so you can engage them quickly.

Strategy #1: Surrender daily
Begin your day by acknowledging you need to fortify your thinking. "Relying on God has to begin all over again every day as if nothing had yet been done."[121] Wake up and release yourself into God's amazing grace—preach yourself the Gospel and start anew in Christ.

> Confidence gives way to Godfidence in the company of God's word.

Strategy #2: Tune into your self-talk—Anchor yourself in God's promises
Actively listen to your inner dialogue loop. Become aware of how your self-talk rises and falls with what is going on in and around you. Pay attention to the direction of your thoughts. By recognizing when your thinking is drifting, you can redirect to God's Word and His promises.

> "The greatest moments in life are the miraculous moments when human impotence and divine omnipotence intersect…who you become is determined by how you pray."

Strategy #3: Read your Bible daily
Confidence gives way to Godfidence in the company of God's word. Focus on and study slices of Scripture. Work with them for weeks—even months—until you have committed them to memory. The Psalmist wrote, "I have hidden your word in my heart that I might not sin against you" (Psalm 119:11, NIV). Create memory aids to bolster your learning—like the coin I mentioned in Chapter 16, with Isaiah 40:28-31 inscribed on it or write the verses on note cards you can pin up or carry with you.

Strategy #4: Start a prayer journal
Prayer focuses your thinking. "The greatest moments in life are the miraculous moments when human impotence and divine omnipotence intersect…who you become is determined by how

you pray. Ultimately, the transcript of your prayers becomes the script of your life."[122] A prayer journal is a powerful way to write a God-honoring script with bold, specific, persistent prayers and having a place to record His faithfulness.

Strategy #5: Turn off the news and manage your social media

If you had a water leak in your home, what would you do? Right, you'd turn off the water. To "take every thought captive and make it obedient to Christ," turn off the news and excuse yourself from the electronic cocktail party that is social media.

Strategy #6: Worship weekly

We were made to worship. In my church, the cross is over the altar, raised high. I think this is significant. I set my gaze upon it by raising my eyes. With our eyes lifted high, we are reminded we are weak and Jesus is strong. God calls us to worship to fortify our thoughts. It is a fortress against the spiritual warfare that is capable of entirely destroying us.

> God calls us to worship to fortify our thoughts.

Strategy #7: Covenant Eyes

The threat of pornography is real. One way to fight it from entering and interfering in your life or the lives of people you love and lead is to use the "Covenant Eyes" (CovenantEyes.com). It was designed to equip people to protect themselves and their families from online dangers.

> Godfidence requires battle readiness—possession of a plan to take every thought captive.

Every day we are engaged in deadly combat with the enemy. Godfidence requires battle readiness—possession of a plan to take every thought captive. Like the fighter pilot, we must grasp it's the 1%—our inner dialogue—that is critical to victory. In the daily dogfight, lean on Paul's encouragement.

> "Whatever is true, whatever is honorable, whatever is right, whatever is pure, whatever is lovely, whatever is

of good repute, if there is any excellence and if anything worthy of praise, dwell on these things. Whatever you have learned or received or heard from me, or seen in me—put it into practice. And the God of peace will be with you."
—Philippians 4:8-9, ESV

CHAPTER 20
PUT FIRST THINGS FIRST

"The Lord cannot fully bless a man until He has first conquered him. The degree of blessing enjoyed by any man will correspond exactly with the completeness of God's victory over him."
—A. W. Tozer

Mortimer Adler collaborated with the President of the University of Chicago, Robert Hutchins, on a project to construct a collection of books that contained the best thinking on the most essential subjects in the history of man.

"Adler and a team of 120 staffers burned through half of the project's $2,000,000 budget compiling an index of the 102 'Great Ideas' that Adler claimed ran through the 443 works the selection committee had chosen to represent the 'Great Conversation of the Western World.'"[123] Adler's work resulted in a collection of 517 essays personifying the most significant achievements in literature, history, law, philosophy, religion, and science. On any theme, you can find out what the great thinkers, philosophers, or writers had to say about a particular topic.

Larry King, the iconic television host, recognizing the collection as one of the most significant publishing feats in history, decided to interview Mortimer Adler. Larry King began, "Mr. Adler, I was looking through the *Great Books of the Western World* to which you were the Editor-In-Chief. Can you tell me why the longest essay is on God? Great themes including history, law, ethics, knowledge, all of this, but God is the longest essay in your compilation. Can you tell me why?"

Mortimer Adler did not hesitate for a moment. He said, "Larry, it's very simple. More consequences for your life follow from that one issue than any other issue you can think of. What you believe or disbelieve in God has everything to do with how you live, why you live, how you orchestrate your life and what your values are."[124]

Adler was not the first guest to be challenged by Larry King about the presence of the living God in our world. Even King, a self-proclaimed atheist,[125] didn't refute Adler's explanation. What priority we give to God in our lives says everything about who we are and how we live.

> What priority we give to God in our lives says everything about who we are and how we live.

Haggai's Timeless Message

Be sure, only one thing can be the center of your life. Our highest priority is easy to spot. It always reflects where we spend our time, talent, and resources. It is impossible for God to be our utmost priority when we operate in *con*fidence. The best we can do is to fit Him in based on the space we make available. Living in Godfidence reflects elevating God to be our highest priority, which prepares us for His anointing and equipping.

> Living in Godfidence reflects elevating God to be our highest priority, which prepares us for His anointing and equipping.

The book of Haggai was written to people who proclaimed God to be their highest priority. They were faithful people who knew God and recognized His voice in their lives. But based on how they were living, you wouldn't have believed they were listening to God—they were lost. I see myself in the story. I think most believers see themselves in the story.

God sent Haggai, His prophet, to remind the people they needed to return to Him—to Godfidently put first things first. The story's background is critical to seeing how *confidence* pushes God off the throne of our lives. The people Haggai was delivering God's message to had returned to Judah from Babylon. They responded to God's call—packed up and relocated their lives. They left well-established and comfortable lives in Babylon. It was home to them, while their Promised Land, decimated by war, was filled with danger and challenges.

They immediately got to work and built an altar. Within two years, they laid the foundation for the Temple—demonstrating God clearly is their highest priority. But without a temple, they got comfortable not having one and turned their attention to building their lives. For the next 14 years, they spent their time, talent, and resources building houses, raising families, and chasing their daily needs. No longer listening for the voice of the Lord, the temple project laid dormant.

Imagine the chatter in their minds. It likely sounded like this, "Hey, I believe rebuilding the Temple is a great cause. Goodness, no one is arguing we shouldn't rebuild it. But things are hectic now—really busy. Remember, the economy has taken a hit. The markets are down. People are struggling. It's just not a good time to spend money we don't have. I'm still going to church—I'm sure God understands my circumstances. We'll back to building the temple as soon as things pick up and money is not so tight."

Haggai delivers a simple message to the people—you forgot to put first things first.

> "This is what the Lord of heavenly forces says, 'These people say, 'The time hasn't come, the time to rebuild the Lord's house.'"
> —Haggai 1:2b, NIV

Everyone was working hard and had less to show for it. They left the temple in ruin—ignored it and went about their business. And while they were looking for God's favor, they didn't make the connection. The provisions and blessing they coveted were not to be found. Haggai pointed out to them that God was fully aware of their circumstances. God was never surprised by the circumstances that confronted them. He created them. God controlled it all—the rain, the land, and the harvest.

> "'You expected much, but see, it turned out to be little. What you brought home, I blew away. Why?' declares the Lord Almighty. 'Because of my house, which remains a ruin, while each of you is busy with your own house.'"
> —Haggai 1:9, NIV

God withheld His blessing because they did not put Him first—"He blew it all away." I'm in this story. You are in this story. In the light of eternity, everything we seek in this world gets turned to dust. When worldly priorities nag at our conscience, as invariably they do, we justify our actions by saying, "Someday I will attend to these eternally important matters, but right now I'm too busy." It's not a matter of teaching. We need to be reminded God is the source of all things! It's not a secret. He takes away to protect and provide for us. There is no significance or fulfillment to anything we pursue that God is not in the center of. Haggai reminds us how Godfidence requires us to put God first regardless of our interpretation of our circumstances.

> **In the light of eternity, everything we seek in this world gets turned to dust.**

Who Do You Love?

When we elevate other relationships or ambition above knowing Jesus and making Him known in the world, we should expect God to blow our *con*fidence away—expose it as a *con*. While social distancing and sheltering was in place during the

COVID-19 pandemic, my wife was texting with a friend. As they exchanged insights and observations, her friend texted, "This has really stripped us of our idols, hasn't it?" She is so right—we are all in the story of Haggai. Everything we were focused on and elevated in importance changed in an instant. "God blew it all away."

James Boice frames up what it means to put first things first, writing, "In the final analysis all inverted priorities are idolatry. They put the creation before the Creator."[126] Putting God first is essential to replacing failing *con*fidence with Godfidence—plugging into the only reliable source of wisdom, courage, and power.

Plugging into Godfidence — Put First Things First

In the process of making a tough career decision, my good friend and mentor Larry Stillman told me, "Jim, if you put your family first, you'll never be disappointed." Larry's wisdom is built upon a principle of Godfidence—if you put God first, you and your family will never be disappointed.

Putting first things first starts by answering two questions.

1. Who do you want to be remembered by?
2. What do you want to be remembered for?

These are temple building questions. Your answers will become the foundation and framework for deciding how you spend your time, talent, and resources. You only finish once (YOFO). Focus, effort, and review are required to finish strong—glorify God and enjoy Him forever. Your answers to these questions direct your attention to where your focus and effort are required. Put first things first. Choose to put God first—you'll never be disappointed.

CHAPTER 21
BUILD A DEEPWATER FAITH

> "The society we live in has not only moved away from a Christian worldview, it has become actively antagonistic toward those who seek to advance faith."[127]
> —David Kinnaman and Gabe Lyons

I wish this statement was simply an opinion. It's easy to discard opinions. Unfortunately, society's shift away from a Christian worldview is not simply an opinion believers can cast aside and not be affected by it. It is the conclusion of a groundbreaking study by Barna Research that explored people's attitudes about faith and religion in the United States.

Preparing to finish strong "in a culture that increasingly thinks practicing Christians are extreme and irrelevant"[128] will require deepwater faith.

Deepwater Faith

One of my favorite musical groups is Casting Crowns. They write and perform bold songs that depict the intersection of faith with the world. I think their song, "Somewhere in the

Middle," describes what living in *con*fidence looks like—getting stuck in shallow faith. The following verse from the lyrics beautifully frames up the dilemma this presents us with:

> "Somewhere between my heart and my hands
> Somewhere between my faith and my plans
> Somewhere between the safety of the
> boat and the crashing waves
> Somewhere between a whisper and a roar
> Somewhere between the altar and the door
> Somewhere between contented peace
> and always wanting more
> Somewhere in the middle you'll find me
>
> Just how close can I get, Lord, to my
> surrender without losing all control.
>
> Fearless warriors in a picket fence, reckless
> abandon wrapped in common sense
> Deepwater faith in the shallow end and
> we are caught in the middle.
> With eyes wide open to the differences, the
> god we want and the God who is
> But will we trade our dreams for His or
> are we caught in the middle."[129]

The Barna research confirmed what I've learned from experience and observation—*con*fident people live in the middle believing they don't need the God who is—the God of the Bible. The pressure from a shifting culture draws confident people into accommodating moral relativism and resisting the absolute truth of God's word. Stuck in the middle, it's easier and more comfortable to blend in with the emerging culture—seek the god we want rather than stand up for the God who is.

Shallow end faith is as deep as *con*fidence allows you to go. It turned me into a spiritual dog paddler. I feared being drawn into deeper water—most of us do. In the shallow end, you grow comfortable thinking about God's sovereignty but not living in the comfort and certainty of its embrace. Be sure, God can't use what we won't give Him. The pride of *con*fidence is a stubborn foe that resists surrender—denying God access to our hearts. Resisting God's desire to do a transformative work within us, we delay (maybe even miss out on) all the extraordinary opportunities He planned for us.

> Be sure, God can't use what we won't give Him. The pride of confidence is a stubborn foe that resists surrender — denying God access to our hearts.

Stand Alone or Fade Away

When our faith collides with popular culture, we are confronted with a choice—stand alone or fade away. Stand alone and you risk being labeled "extreme." Fade away and you accept your faith as being "irrelevant." Be sure the enemy's goal is for us to stand on our own and fade away. Satan doesn't want us to develop a deepwater faith that emboldens us to stand up for Jesus and live courageously in His power.

> Godfidence — standing on God's truth — enables us to stand alone when our faith collides with popular culture.

"Be sober-minded; be watchful. Your adversary
the devil prowls around like a roaring
lion, seeking someone to devour."
—1 Peter 5:8, ESV

Godfidence—standing on God's truth—enables us to stand alone when our faith collides with popular culture. Standing alone means we are willing to stand up and be counted—proclaim the Gospel; praise God in good times and bad; work independently on challenging assignments, and raise God up in our lives. Standing alone is a quality of deepwater faith that emboldens us to speak truth in love because of the hope we have in Christ.

More Than Conquerors

Studying the 8th chapter of Paul's letter to the Romans is instructive in developing deepwater faith. This was one of the places along this journey to Godfidence that God taught me the importance of slowing down. I read and studied this chapter for months—actively circling, underlining, and taking notes. I encourage you to slow down for a moment too. Set aside any familiarity you have with these passages and explore them with fresh eyes and a heart open to hear God's voice.

Paul begins in verse 30 by assuring us of the love God made available to us through Jesus.

> "And those whom he predestined he also called,
> and those whom he called he also justified, and
> those whom he justified he also glorified."
> —Romans 8:30, ESV

Given the strength and atoning power of Jesus, Paul then tees up two critical questions to developing the deepwater faith that breeds Godfidence.

> "What then shall we say to these things? If
> God is for us, who can be against us?"
> —Romans 8:31, ESV

"If God is for us, who can be against us" is an awe-inspiring battle cry. Because I'd heard this amazing promise countless times, I had to ask myself, why was I still insisting on standing on my own? I wrestled with this question for a long time. I had to accept that at best, I dabbled on the fringes of what Jesus did for me and you on the cross. But, day-by-day, as I read this passage, God revealed that my confidence defeated me because I never fully embraced and accepted the unmerited gift of His grace.

The freedom from *con*fidence I longed for started to emerge when I began contemplating the privilege Jesus affords me and you, laid out by Paul in verses 32-34:

> "He who did not spare his own Son, but gave him up for us all—how will he not also, along with him, graciously give us all things? It is God who justifies. Who then is the one who condemns? No one. Christ Jesus who died—more than that, who was raised to life—is at the right hand of God and is also interceding for us."

Now, it no longer escaped me that Jesus, who died and was raised to life, intercedes for me every day. He is interceding for you too. Relying upon Jesus to intercede for us is a cornerstone of Godfidence. Paul continues building this incredible foundation of deepwater faith in verse 35:

> **Relying upon Jesus to intercede for us is a cornerstone of Godfidence.**

> "Who shall separate us from the love of Christ?"

The answer to this question draws us into deeper water. It connects us to the only reliable source of confidence in the world—Jesus.

> "Shall trouble or hardship or persecution or famine or nakedness or danger or sword? As it is written: 'For your sake we face death all day long; we are considered as sheep to be slaughtered.' No, in all these things we are more than conquerors through him who loved us. For I am convinced that neither death nor life, neither angels nor demons, neither the present nor the future, nor any powers, neither height nor depth, nor anything else in all creation, will be able to separate us from the love of God that is in Christ Jesus our Lord."
> —Romans 8:35b-39, NIV

We can be Godfident amidst the changing tides of culture because we are more than conquerors through him who loved us. Breathe that in for a moment. We can affect the depth of our relationship with Jesus Christ. We can grow more reliant on the relationship. We can assign value to the relationship. But nothing we ever do can rob us of the love Christ has for us. Deepwater faith sparks the Godfidence to stand alone because we are standing on the strength and power of our Risen Lord.

No Surprises

Why am I Godfident? Why should you be Godfident? In Christ, we no longer have to fight for our future. When we embrace this eternal gift a deepwater faith is sure to grow within us. You see, God knows what lies ahead of us. He planned for it. "Knowing the future, even the future of human decisions, is part of what it means to be God."[130] God is in our past, in our present, and our future. Nothing has or will surprise Him. He is actively directing and guarding all of our ways.

Plugging into Godfidence — Building Deepwater Faith

In closing out this chapter, I am going to outline some deepwater faith tools. The road to finishing strong will likely be more antagonistic than we could ever imagine. Looking onto the horizon, it is not a journey to be walked alone. Walking alone means standing on our own, which causes us to lose our Godfidence for all the wrong reasons.

> God is in our past, in our present, and our future. Nothing has or will surprise Him. He is actively directing and guarding all of our ways.

You can build and reinforce deepwater faith by actively engaging in Christian community.

> "Therefore, since we are surrounded by such a great cloud of witnesses, let us throw off everything that hinders and the sin that so easily entangles. And let us run with perseverance the race marked out for us, fixing our eyes on Jesus…"
> —Hebrews 12:1-2a, NIV

Christian community is a gift that comes from the connection we share in Jesus. It produces deepwater faith that strengthens, preserves, and encourages us in all seasons and circumstances of life. When we engage in worship, Bible studies, small groups, mentoring relationships, and outreach ministries, we give God time and space to prepare and equip us to be impactful and relevant culture shapers.

Seeking and engaging in Christian community helped heal me. Being in the company of a Biblically-grounded, Christ-centric community, you will:

- Honor God.
- Grow in Biblical wisdom.
- Receive encouragement and support.
- Be supported and comforted in prayer.
- Discover the depth and breadth of your spiritual gifts.
- Prepare your heart for service.
- Grow in compassion for people.
- Learn how to forgive and receive forgiveness.
- See your identity in Christ.
- Embrace a spirit of teachability.
- Become a living witness to the Gospel.
- Grow in Godfidence.

Remember, it is not necessary to fight for the outcome. The victory is already won. We possess the deepwater faith necessary to stand alone based on Godfidence, which comes from Christ alone.

> "You, dear children, are from God and have overcome them, because the one who is in you is greater than the one who is in the world."
> —1 John 4:4, NIV

CHAPTER 22
KEEP YOUR EYE ON THE FINISH LINE

"There is no magic in small plans. When I consider my ministry, I think of the world. Anything less than that would not be worthy of Christ nor of His will for my life."
—Henrietta Mears

Henrietta Mears had the most far-reaching impact on the conduct of ministry of any woman of the twentieth century.[131] In the summer of 1949, she invited a young preacher to speak at a Christian retreat center she founded in the San Bernardino Mountains of California.

Billy Graham showed up at Forest Homes discouraged and full of questions. He called his most recent crusade, "a flop." To complicate things, Henrietta was being criticized for inviting Billy to speak. She stood steadfast in her invitation to have Billy preach and provided vital encouragement to him during his stay.

One night Billy laid his hand across his Bible and lifted this prayer, "Father, I am going to accept this as Thy Word—by faith! I'm going to allow faith to go beyond my intellectual questions and doubts, and I will believe this to be Your inspired Word!" At that moment, he said he felt the power and presence of God in a way he hadn't in months, noting, "A major bridge had been crossed."[132] The next day, 400 people made a new commitment to Christ after Billy preached. "He preached with authority," according to Henrietta Mears.

The historic 1949 Los Angeles Crusade followed just a few weeks later. Billy Graham would preach to thousands of people who packed the Crusade's "Canvas Cathedral." It was here that Billy Graham led Louis Zamperini to surrender his life to Christ. The Crusade scheduled for three weeks ended up running for eight weeks and catapulted Billy into the national spotlight. Billy Graham's remarkable evangelistic ministry pivoted in the company of one woman who was committed to finishing well—finishing strong.

It's One Thing

The mindset of finishing strong awakens—transforming our thinking—when we set our eyes on eternity. Keeping our eyes fixed on the finish line assures the most critical thing in our lives is always in front of us. I frequently wondered why I struggled to see this vital connection. After much reflection, I can say it's one thing. If the idea of being welcomed into the arms of Jesus doesn't cause our hearts to swell with joy and anticipation, then we don't know Jesus. Knowing who Jesus is and pursuing Him are two entirely different things. Knowing Christ personally—accepting His redeeming grace and embracing the gift of eternity that awaits us—is the wellspring of Godfidence.

> "See what great love the Father has lavished on us, that we should be called children of God! And that is what we are! The reason the world does not know us is that it did not know him."
> —1 John 3:1, NIV

When we seek Jesus with our whole heart, we will come to know Him in Spirit and in truth. Henrietta Mears made it her daily pursuit to know Jesus and share Him with everyone she met. She was asked near the end of her life what she would have done differently. The woman who trained and mentored Billy Graham, Bill Bright—Founder of Campus Crusade for Christ, Dawson Trotman—Founder of Navigators, Jim Rayborn—Founder of Young Life, Richard Halvorson—U. S. Senate Chaplain and Chairman of World Vision, and Ronald Reagan—the 40th President of the United States, said, "I would have trusted Christ more."[133]

> However great our dreams might be, they will always be less than what God is capable of doing in us and through us.

Do the Work

I am sure we can't comprehend the depth of the talent God has planted inside of us. However great our dreams might be, they will always be less than what God is capable of doing in us and through us. Wrap your head around that for a moment. Within you are the seeds of significant Kingdom impact. Seeds that are essential to completing the assignments God gives us. Seeds we must allow Him to nurture if we are going to finish strong.

It may be hard to accept, but each of us is where we are at this moment in our lives by God's appointment or allowance. We must embrace the fact that God gives us our assignments based on His priorities and not our preferences. We may not like the task—even want to reject it because we think it should be more or different. Have no doubt; there are no insignificant or inferior assignments in God's economy. Each one is important to His redemptive plan and our role in it. Ignore your age, experience, position, and condition. He will give us everything we need to finish strong. "I am convinced and confident of this very thing, that He who has begun a good work in you will

> We must embrace the fact that God gives us our assignments based on His priorities and not our preferences.

[continue to] perfect and complete it until the day of Christ Jesus [the time of His return]."¹³⁴

> God is more than enough. He will assuredly provide all that is required to fulfill whatever He places on our hearts to do. We simply need to do the work.

Let's personalize this—what would you do if you knew you couldn't fail? Easy—you'd take massive action. This is the mindset of Godfidence. *Con*fidence engulfs us in the false belief that we need something more before taking action—more knowledge, more money, more time, more support, more applause, or more appreciation. God is more than enough. He will assuredly provide all that is required to fulfill whatever He places on our hearts to do. We simply need to do the work.

OPPORTUNITYISNOWHERE

The majority of people who read this say, "Opportunity is no where." Instead, what if you had eyes to see, "Opportunity is now here." God wants you to see the future He has planned for you with fresh eyes. It is God who places dreams on our hearts that are ripe with life-giving and life-changing opportunities. What if you acted on the dreams He places on your heart, invested the effort, and let Him lead? "Whatever you do [whatever your task may be], work from the soul [that is, put in your very best effort], as [something done] for the Lord and not for men" (Colossians 3:23, AMP). Keeping your eye on the finish line inspires the effort that builds our Godfidence and paves the path to finish strong.

Finishing Well Formula

We are always free to choose the level of our effort. God plants the seeds and assigns the fields. Our effort is the multiplier that produces the harvest. Think of it as the "finishing strong formula."

- (Seeds of Talent) x (Effort) = Spiritual gift development
- (Spiritual gifts) x (Effort) = Serving
- (Serving) x (Effort) = God honoring impact—completing your assignments

Making an effort is an act of obedience that releases God's most excellent assistance and blessing. Idleness is never an assignment. As hard as it may be to admit, taking up residence in a lounge chair is a choice. Idleness takes hold of us when we take our eye off the finish line. The *con*fident person falsely believes the finish line is a distant destination—sensing no urgency to act. The Godfident person has their eye on the finish line—"working out their salvation with fear and trembling" (Philippians 2:12b, NIV).

We should act as if we are closer to the finish than we think. "The Parable of the Rich Fool" provides the perfect reference point. "The rich man said, 'Soul, you have ample goods laid up for many years; relax, eat, drink, be merry.' But God said to him, 'Fool! This night your soul is required of you, and the things you have prepared, whose will they be?'" (Luke 12:19-20, ESV). Fixing your eyes on the finish line gives rise to an incessant desire to prepare as if each day was your last—filling your heart with the desire to finish strong.

> **We should act as if we are closer to the finish than we think.**

Let's talk about the fact that we'll face a few character-building assignments along the way. We may not like them, but it's God's way of assuring our character keeps pace with our accomplishments. Accepting victories and completing tough assignments in humility keeps our eyes fixed on the finish line. The advice here is demanding and straightforward. Stick with your assignments to the finish—bad jobs, insignificant jobs, demanding jobs, thankless jobs, marriages, parenting, caring for aging parents—embrace whatever God assigns. Allow Him to lead you through.

Plugging into Godfidence — Keep Your Eye on the Finish Line

Miracles pivot on the work of a single man or woman who keeps their eyes fixed on the finish line. Do you think Henrietta Mears knew Billy Graham would become the most influential evangelist of this century? Do you think Billy Graham knew that he would lead Louis Zamperini to embrace the grace of Jesus? Do you think Louis Zamperini knew God would use his suffering to open Victory Boys Camp and pour love and grace into thousands of "at-risk" boys? We have no idea what God purposes through the assignments He gives us.

> Miracles pivot on the work of a single man or woman who keeps their eyes fixed on the finish line.

When we accept God's assignments, we are stepping into Godfidence. Looking through history a story emerges that reveals the Christians who have had the most impact on the current world were just those who have their eyes on the next—finishing strong. Stretch your imagination. What do you see being accomplished if you trusted Christ every day and focused on being who God created you to be—nothing more and nothing less? Embracing the fact that it's not your job to produce your life's story produces freedom and Godfidence. It's your job to play the part God assigned to you in the most extraordinary love story ever written.

> Embracing the fact that it's not your job to produce your life's story produces freedom and Godfidence.

Lord, give me ears to hear your guiding voice. Spark within me an urgency to act on the dreams you place on my heart. Grant me the humility to embrace the assignments you give me and the strength and wisdom to finish them. Help me to know you more, bring you glory in all I do, and to rest at the end of each day, knowing I gave you my best effort. Amen.

My prayer is you'll use this prayer to help you keep your eyes on the finish line.

PART FIVE
FINISHING STRONG

"I believe my future is greater than my past."

Who do you picture when you read these words? Did you see someone sitting in a wheelchair? Imagine someone who can't speak? Identify someone dependent on people and technology to function? Can you imagine someone who fits this description leading a cutting edge organization committed to improving lives?

Steve Gleason uttered these words in 2016. I've been a fan of Steve's for a long time. He grew up in my hometown, and we both attended Washington State University, which is where the similarities end. Steve was a decorated student-athlete at Gonzaga Prep High School. He was a star linebacker on Washington State's 1998 Rose Bowl team and a four-year starter on the WSU baseball team.

Steve played six years in the NFL for the New Orleans Saints. On September 26, 2006, the rebuilt Superdome and the city of New Orleans hosted an NFL game for the first time since Hurricane Katrina. Steve is closely identified with the city's resurgence because his blocked punt—that turned into a

New Orleans touchdown—sparked a Saints victory. This play etched his name into Saints lore and is commemorated with a statue entitled "Rebirth."

Steve's life was unfolding like a storybook collection of personal and professional success. Then in 2011, he was diagnosed with ALS (Lou Gehrig's disease—amyotrophic lateral sclerosis). Now facing a diagnosis that came with a life expectancy of two to five years,[135] Steve's path to finishing strong immediately turned down a road filled with daunting physical and emotional challenges.

In 2016, Steve was invited by the Archdiocese of New Orleans, to speak about his faith. With the use of eye-tracking software that produces a computerized voice, Steve began by saying, "I didn't realize I would be this emotional when I was asked to speak several weeks ago. I hesitantly said yes. I don't think I've ever spoken publicly about my beliefs on God or religion. Furthermore when the Archdiocese asked me to speak about my personal faith, I grew more tentative and reluctant… As soon as a person speaks publicly about their personal faith, their faith is no longer personal."[136]

Talking about his faith, Steve said, "In the beginning stages, I certainly prayed to be healed. I also saw healing on nearly every level. My seeking healing was by faith…I rarely pray to be healed these days. Maybe I have lost some faith—who knows. While I would like to walk and talk again, the Creator can choose to heal me or not. Most importantly, I enjoy my life…I pray for my daily bread, my strength, and my ingenuity to continue living the life I love with purpose."[137]

Steve frequently hears, "Oh Steve, this is such a tragedy what's happened" with your diagnosis. But Steve is not inclined to focus on his condition or see the world through the lens of what others perceive to be limitations. "He's driven to say, 'What can we do to turn that tragedy into heroics?'"[138] Steve believes the most important word in his vocabulary is "purpose," which is reflected in his motto, "No white flags!" Steve says, "The truth is that we all experience pain in our lives, but I believe the problems we face are our opportunity to find our human purpose."¹³⁹ By 2019, "Team Gleason" provided almost $10 million in adventure, technology, equipment, and care services to over 15,000 people living with ALS and countless others through advocacy, support, and ultimately bringing an end to the disease.¹⁴⁰

On January 15, 2020, Steve received the Congressional Gold Medal of Honor—the highest civilian award in the United States—in recognition of his contributions. Drew Brees, the future Hall of Fame quarterback of the New Orleans Saints and Steve's teammate, spoke at the White House ceremony. He told the story receiving an email from Steve, informing him of his diagnosed condition. Steve wrote, "I promise to fight and believe. And expect the extraordinary. And smile, and laugh, and love our lives for every breath that remains in my body. Please, please, please help me do that until I am 109."¹⁴¹

No white flags. Steve is God's handiwork. Therefore, no one can do what God calls Steve to do. Our earthly perspective makes it difficult to embrace the fact that God prepared Steve for this assignment. Everything in his past prepared him for these challenging days. I'm sure Steve didn't ask God for this assignment. No one would. But God prepared him for it, as demonstrated by how he has purposefully lived it out.

What About You?

Is your future greater than your past? You can be Godfident that's God's plan for you. You are God's handiwork (Philippians 2:10)—priceless in His eyes. The self-description Paul uses to open his letter to the Romans is instructive as to being Godfident about your future.

> "Paul, a <u>servant of Christ Jesus,</u> <u>called</u> to be an apostle and <u>set apart</u> for the gospel of God—"
> —Romans 1:1, NIV

Paul's description applies to all who claim God's grace in Jesus' redeeming work on the cross and proclaim Him as Lord. Paul uses three descriptors.

1. We are servants of Jesus. Serving is core to our identity in Christ.

2. We are called. Our service is defined by God's divinely appointed assignments. Every role, vocation, or circumstance of our life is our uniquely assigned mission field.

3. We are potentially set apart by God to complete a specific assignment.

The experiences and paths of your life represent the threads God uses to weave together a tapestry that ultimately becomes the picture of your life. Knowing it is His hand at work gives rise to our Godfidence.

Finishing Strong

Your value in and to the world cannot be fulfilled by anyone but you. In Part Five, we'll focus on the finish line. Lean in knowing no one has your unique time and place in the world to positively impact the people God purposefully places in your path—no one! In Christ, your future is always greater than your past. Every day is a good day to focus on finishing strong.

> **Your value in and to the world cannot be fulfilled by anyone but you.**

CHAPTER 23
MAKE ROOM FOR GOD TO SURPRISE YOU

"Not only that, but we rejoice in our sufferings, knowing that suffering produces endurance, and endurance produces character, and character produces hope."
—Romans 5:3-4, ESV

What do you remember about the year 2020? Even if you enthusiastically waved goodbye to 2020, it's hard to imagine that its tumultuous events didn't continue to touch your life for years to come. I saw a t-shirt that summed up how most people remember it. Emblazoned across the chest was "2020," along with five stars like you see when asked to provide a product review. One of the five stars was filled in gold. Below was the comment, "Very bad, would not recommend."

I entered 2020 with a full heart and clarity of purpose. By February 1, I had finished writing almost everything you've read to this point. My plan to publish this book in June, on my 61st birthday, was coming together. I didn't consider, for even a moment, that God would present me with a detour. The best way to describe the change of plans is we had two prayers collide. While we prayed for guidance and inspiration for this book, we were also prayerfully considering a move to the state of Washington to be closer to family. Despite pouring myself into researching, writing, editing, and ultimately seeing God's hand move in this work, my wife, Kristi, and I felt assured now was the time to move.

Goodbye Sunny and 75°

Setting my writing aside to prepare for the sale of our home of 18 years wasn't easy. It breathed life back into the *con*fident me and gave rise to a voice that screamed, "Press on and finish this book." I tried to keep writing. But when I sat down to write, my thoughts were empty. In frustration, I pushed God to tell me, "Why?" My confusion about why He brought me this far and then asked me to set it aside did not prompt a reply. Adding to my frustration was the fact I love 75 degrees and sunny. Having lived in Southern California for nearly 40 years, I had difficulty thinking a move to dark, wet, and windy winter days was my next best move. It might be God's, but it wasn't mine.

Then as if I needed another reason to question God's wisdom and pump the brakes on a move, the coronavirus threw a dark blanket over the world. I wanted to believe this was God's way of telling us to postpone this move. Be sure, this was all me—the *con*fident, I'm in charge, me speaking for God. In all honesty, this move was pushing me to do things I selfishly did not want to do. Given we had no idea what to expect going forward in the uncertainty surrounding COVID-19, avoiding its obvious challenges made complete sense to me.

Who Knew?

The Godfident me knew we needed to make this move. It didn't mean we wouldn't be challenged or have to endure some suffering—we would. But as it is with trusting God's direction and provision, we would be journeying beneath the umbrella of His safety and protection. When the first family to view our home wrote an offer, we welcomed it as God's provision. Shortly after the appraisal and inspection were completed, the Governor of California issued shelter-in-place orders—businesses shut down, schools closed, churches shuttered their doors, and real estate open houses were eliminated. The ensuing fear added a level of uncertainty that would make this move even more challenging, starting with discovering that cold feet was a COVID-19 symptom—who knew? Our buyer, succumbing to this frosty condition, backed out of the purchase.

With no clear direction on how to show our home, we paused our listing. After a couple weeks with no end to the lockdown in sight, we went back on the market. Nearly immediately, God provided another buyer. This was great news but would require us to pack up and be out of the house in 30 days—time to move on! Simultaneously, the virus was turning emptying grocery store shelves and the hoarding of cleaning supplies, paper towels, and toilet paper into a sport. Our concern about winning the "War for Charmin" paled compared to what orchestrating a long-distance household move entailed.

We immediately discovered a difference between getting a moving company to quote the move and a moving company that would commit to packing and transporting our goods in the required time frame. We would have loved to turn to friends. Many were eager to help us pack, clean, run errands, and welcome us to stay with them. But given how little we knew about the virus, they were hesitant to assist us (we understood). Add to the list of unknowns was the fact that finding a new home was no sure thing. For-sale home inventory was scarce in the area of Seattle we were looking at. Potential homes of interest were selling over the asking price the day they went on the market. Oh, and by the way, that little 1,200-mile drive would take us through three states that had shut down hotels, restaurants, and rest areas.

Confidence Knocks on the Door — Again

The lack of answers clouded my thinking. Frequently, I wondered, "Why are we doing this?" This question stuck in my mind like velcro. As it pressed Godfidence down in favor of my *con*fidence, I came up with more reasons to abort the move. Start with the fact my wife had an incredible group of godly women in her life. How about we were knit together in a small group with three other encouraging, faith-filled couples. Don't overlook the fact that we were members of a wonderful church community. Hey, what about all the wonderful friends we loved and leaned on over nearly 40 years? Throw in it's 75 degrees and sunny almost every day (yes, I said it again), and I had all the reasons I needed to ask, "Why?"

In chapter 10, I said, "In the enemy's hands, we ask, 'Why?'" When we focus on understanding why countless unexplainable things happen in our lives, it prompts us to question God's providential hand. I'm pretty sure I'll never completely stop asking, "Why?" None of us will. But what I was beginning to realize was that our spiritual journey is filled with a persistent struggle between self-reliant *con*fidence and living in the strength and protection of Godfidence. Our move amid 2020 craziness—COVID-19, politics, elections, riots, and fires—exemplified this tension.

Thank you, Lord!

God shredded my *con*fidence as He opened doors. We secured a moving company, a car transport company, and every resource we needed to close the sale of our home. The last hurdle was securing a new home. After making two unsuccessful offers, we were less than 30 days away from arriving in Washington. It appeared that the window of time to complete a purchase and avoid putting our goods in storage had closed. Then, on a Saturday morning, our son and realtor, Scott, said they found a new listing that might work. Like all the others, it was going to go fast. With no time to fly up to inspect the home, we relied on conversation, pictures, and videos. We learned enough to write a full-price offer we hoped the sellers would accept immediately. The house had only been on the market a few hours when Scott informed us that our offer was one of five presented to the sellers, and three were higher than ours.

After Scott and I talked through a couple of counter-offer scenarios, the *con*fident me pressed to take over. All I could think was, "Don't lose this house, Jim. Just increase the offer and finish this." But Kristi, ever faithful, kept me from exerting my will on the process. We turned to God again—asking Him to guide our decision. After talking about our options, we prayed for direction. We informed Scott we weren't going to offer more money, but instead would drop all contingencies. Scott felt it was unlikely the sellers would accept our offer without raising our price. But he assured us he would do his best to gain acceptance. He was right. There was no apparent reason for the seller to forgo a higher selling price. But God had a different reply—the sellers accepted our offer.

This should have been the end to this story of God's amazing provision. Everything pointed to a clear and easy path to close. But to our surprise, the struggle wasn't over. Just days before our closing date, our home loan fell apart. Because I had been in daily contact with the lender, we were caught completely off guard. They assured us everything was in order—right up to the point when they backed out of the deal. Now just days away from closing, I contacted the lender we didn't originally choose—pleading with them to take this on. Unfortunately, there was not enough time for them to process and fund the loan. We floated the idea of extending the escrow to the seller. Their response left no room for negotiation—close on the agreed-upon date, or they would pursue another buyer.

This was a test of Godfidence. On my journey to lean on God for all provision and wisdom (reliable confidence), God peeled back the layers of my *con*fidence. He allowed me to see who I truly am—who we all are—weak, vulnerable, and dependent upon Him. This was one of those "Ask" moments—pray with holy anticipation and expectation. What emerged was a single option to secure the monies we needed to close. It presented us with three significant barriers. It was unconventional, difficult, and unlikely. When this highly improbable option became a reality, it would have been just like my suppressed *con*fident self to claim the victory and celebrate what I had done. Instead, only three Godfident words were appropriate, "Thank you, Lord."

The Rest of the Story

Retracing my steps and thinking about God's provision in this seemingly impossible circumstance impressed upon me that there is a persistent spiritual struggle between *con*fidence and Godfidence. It's real. I wish I could tell you that Godfidence eliminates obstacles, minimizes challenges, and wipes away pain and suffering—it doesn't.

The Bible begins with paradise being thrust into suffering. From here on, short of being welcomed into eternity, there is nothing in Scripture to suggest our lives will be free of suffering. It's an inescapable part of our human condition. Suffering is where this book began. God used it to develop my reliance upon Him. It's necessary to develop spiritual maturity. Every road to Godfidence either begins or passes through suffering. When God asked me to set the completion of this book aside in February of 2020, I had no idea He would show me, once again, who He is and write the close to this book.

Upon arriving in Washington, the reasons for being near our family quickly emerged. First, there was awesome news. Our oldest son, Matthew, and his lovely wife, Abby, brought us a housewarming gift. Inside the beautifully wrapped package was a handprinted sign. It reads, "Only the Best Parents Get Promoted to Grandparents." Oh, the joy to be able to be part of Paige Mackenzie's life. No big reveal parties necessary—it's a girl! And then there was the not so good news. My mom was diagnosed with vascular dementia. Her condition made it necessary to move her out of her home in Spokane. The process of getting her settled in Seattle in the face of COVID-19 has been challenging—the story is still unfolding. We didn't see this coming, but God did. It's just like Him to know where we are needed before we do.

How we react in light of unforeseen and untimely suffering reveals our focus. We either gaze upon Jesus and are strengthened in Godfidence or looking within—quaking in fear of our failed confidence. In Christ, we can be Godfident in the face of suffering. He calls us to cast our gaze upon Him, saying, "I have said these things to you, that in me you may have peace. In the world you will have tribulation. But take heart; I have overcome the world" (John 16:33, ESV). Godfidence embraces the wonder of God. It leaves room for God to come into our lives at any time in unexpected ways and surprise us with His goodness, mercy, and love.

> "For I am confident of this very thing, that He who began a good work in you will perfect it until the day of Christ Jesus."
> —Philippians 1:6, NASB

CHAPTER 24
ONE-ON-ONE WITH JESUS

"Remember how short my life is; remember that you created all of us mortal! Who can live and never die? How can human beings keep themselves from the grave?"
—Psalm 89:47-48, TLB

Our exploration of Godfidence is almost complete. Godfidence reflects my best attempt to embrace the fact YOFO (you only finish once) and thus describe how to fulfill the desperate desire to finish well that naturally flows from within us (Ecclesiastes 3:11). We can't escape the divine DNA embedded within our hearts that yearns for a Savior. Brokenness and pain turned my world upside down—sending me scurrying for answers. Godfidence emerged as I sought God with my whole heart. Be sure, reliable confidence—Godfidence—can only be discovered in union with God. It encourages us to put on the complete armor of God[142], so we can resist and stand our ground against the enemy. Godfidence embodies what is required to lean into the future with purpose and urgency—full of faith, holy expectation, and obedience.

When I invited you to join me on this journey to Godfidence, I stated that if you desired to finish well, finish strong, you were in the right place. Knowing in the next few minutes you will put this book down—maybe never to pick it up again, I can't let you go without asking—do you now know with certainty how to finish strong? We don't make it a habit to think about the finish line of our life. The foolish and unbelieving think they'll always see the sun come up tomorrow—life will go on forever. It won't. Our days are numbered. Our lives are short. The essential truth is that every day we open our eyes is a gift from our Creator.

> **Godfidence embodies what is required to lean into the future with purpose and urgency—full of faith, holy expectation, and obedience.**

David grasped the brevity of life. "Let me know my end, Lord. How many days do I have left? I want to know how brief my time is" (Psalm 39:4). David had his eyes firmly fixed on the finish line, knowing his life and reign as King were limited. Job lived the prime of his life in the grip of torment and loss. His ten children were killed in an accident. He was stripped of his wealth and worldly standing. He was stricken with illness and cast out of his home. Even his own wife told him to curse the Lord. But Job's commitment to Lord never wavered. Job 14:5 gives us perspective on his sustained love for God. "Our time on earth is brief; the number of our days is already decided by You." Job knew God's character perfectly. He understood his struggles would be brief in light of eternity. Our days are numbered, "Therefore do not worry about tomorrow, for tomorrow will worry about itself. Each day has enough trouble of its own" (Matthew 6:34). Today is the decisive day.

> **The foolish and unbelieving think they'll always see the sun come up tomorrow—life will go on forever. It won't. Our days are numbered. Our lives are short.**

Do You Believe?

"There is much about death we do not know. God hasn't chosen to answer all our questions about it."[143] But contemplating the consequences of death is important for two reasons. First, it establishes the framework for how you'll choose to live today. Second, it confronts you with a vital question, "How did you respond to Jesus?" Both are important, but your response to Jesus says everything anyone wants or needs to know about you. It's going to happen—you draw your last breath, your heart stops beating, and your earthly life is over. Now what? Only one question remains. Do you believe?

"The nature of that belief, the significance of that belief, the sum and substance of that belief is far more than an intellectual awareness of the existence of a Jesus of Nazareth. It means the casting of myself upon, it means the relying of myself upon, it means entrusting all of my life and all of my eternity into the hands of Jesus of Nazareth, believing that he is the person that he claimed to be."[144]

Believing Jesus is the exclusive Savior of the world is opposed to the increasingly popular world view that all religious faiths are equal. This perceived kinder and gentler approach to faith and religion sets truth aside in favor of inclusiveness and tolerance. Today's mainstream narrative is that Christians should know better than to claim Jesus is the only way to God because all faith paths lead to God. This is a problem. Jesus is not an option among many. He didn't offer us that choice.

Jesus is not an option among many. He didn't offer us that choice.

> "Let not your hearts be troubled. Believe in God; believe also in me. In my Father's house are many rooms. If it were not so, would I have told you that I go to prepare a place for you? And if I go and prepare a place for you, I will come again and will take you to myself, that where I am you may be also. And you know the way to where I am going." Thomas said to him, 'Lord, we do not know

where you are going. How can we know the way?' Jesus said to him, 'I am the way, and the truth, and the life. No one comes to the Father except through me.'"
—John 14:1-6, NIV

Godfidence is an invitation to faith in Christ—The One who is the way, the truth, and the life. It's not a guide to help you look Christian on the outside—reframing the God who is into the god you want Him to be on the inside. Godfidence recognizes that "the world—the totality of humanity that is set in opposition to God—is constantly seeking to conform us to its own standards and values."[145] Godfidence requires surrendering to Jesus—accepting God's eternal salvation. It's the only way to finishing strong. Do you believe?

Godfidence grows in the fertile soil of the gospel. If we get disconnected from the promise and power of the gospel, Godfidence is lost. The power of the gospel cannot be overstated. It is the greatest exchange in all of human history. We lay our sins upon Christ in exchange for His righteousness. "For our sake he made him to be sin who knew no sin, so that in him we might become the righteousness of God" (2 Corinthians 5:21). We need to preach the vital truth of the gospel to ourselves every day to embolden our Godfidence. Be reminded, the power that brought Jesus into this world and raised Him to life after death is the same power that resides with every believer. (Galatians 2:20)

> **Godfidence grows in the fertile soil of the gospel. If we get disconnected from the promise and power of the gospel, Godfidence is lost.**

Just Imagine!

Take a step over the finish line for a moment. Imagine being welcomed into the arms of Jesus. Pause here for a moment—be still. Think about the great exchange that took place to secure your salvation. I envision being overwhelmed by the enormity of this moment. One-on-one with Jesus—quivering in awe as

I stand in the presence of the One who took the judgment I deserved upon Himself in order for me to worship and enjoy Him forever. Now bring your focus back to this moment—today. Every breath you take a reminder that the ordained cause of Christ God has assigned to you remains before you. Henry Martyn, an Anglican chaplain and a missionary, said, "You are immortal until God's purpose for you is complete."[146]

> "For it is [not your strength, but it is] God who is effectively at work in you, both to will and to work [that is, strengthening, energizing, and creating in you the longing and the ability to fulfill your purpose] for His good pleasure."
> —Philippians 2:13, AMP

I can assure you I don't know what I am doing or where I am going in the days that lie ahead. My journey to Godfidence helped me realize I don't need to. Neither do you because God does. It doesn't mean I don't get anxious—I do. I'm thankful for the strength He gives me to be still and listen for His voice and follow where He leads me. It hasn't completely stopped me from asking Him to tell me what He's going to do next and what He wants me to do. Some days are harder than others to surrender all—give Him my heart, and mind, and allow Him to lead. But I believe—His way is perfect and His provision always on time.

I pray this journey to Godfidence has helped you, as much as it did me, more fully understand God's character and nature—how He loves us and desires to bring us to Himself. Oswald Chambers captures the essence of the journey beautifully, writing, "When God gets us alone through suffering, heartbreak, temptation, disappointment, sickness, or thwarted desires, a broken friendship, or a new friendship—when He gets us absolutely alone, and we are totally speechless, unable to ask even one question, then He begins to teach us."[147]

As you embark on your own journey to Godfidence, I pray God fills you with the courage to live Godfidently in the shadow of the finish line. Be sure, you can't love Jesus too much. You can't think about Him too much, or thank Him too much, or depend upon Him too much. All our forgiveness, all our justification, all our righteousness is in Christ. Welcome each day as a gift. Lean in with urgency. God is calling you to finish strong. I believe. I pray you do too.

ACKNOWLEDGMENTS

My Wife

Kristi, you read the introduction and said, "Where was I? How did I miss this?" You were right there every step of the way. Your passion for what is true, pure, and God-honoring inspires me. Your presence, support, and encouragement always shape my thinking and guide me to set my gaze on Jesus. Godfidence is the fruit of your love.

My Mom

Throughout writing Godfidence, I thought of my mom frequently. She laid the foundation for my faith in Christ. She is a beacon of God's love and grace that never dims.

Readers, Editors, and Truth Tellers

This project was blessed by a variety of people who came alongside me during the concept development and writing of

Godfidence. I am forever grateful for your investment of time and the belief you gave me that this was a worthwhile project.

- Jim Ireland, friend seems insufficient. Your steady and reliable voice has been a weekly constant in my life for years. We came together in the most unlikely of circumstances. Looking back I am overwhelmed with thanks thinking of the many ways in which God has blessed our journey—thank you!

- Vera Reidy, your heart for the Lord, rings out in everything you do. The depth of your Biblical knowledge and eye for what makes a story work helped to shape this book.

- Carole Samuels, you are a voice I listen to. Your kindness and love for the Lord are qualities I admire. You provided so many keen insights that gave this book a new dimensions. There wouldn't have been a study guide if it weren't for you.

- John Harrison, you are a warrior for the Lord. You pushed me to teach from *Godfidence* before publishing and put the study guide to the test. Thank you for being a voice of encouragement.

- Ed Ewart, you helped me shape the message. Your pastoral eye and Biblical knowledge provided needed direction and support. You are a great example of what the journey to the finish line should look like.

- Terrie Squire, you have been reading my writing for years. The stories in Godfidence have broad appeal because you guided me to see the need and write to it. No one prays with more passion and persistence than you—thank you for praying for this work and contributing to it.

ACKNOWLEDGMENTS

- <u>Rich and Patty Green</u>, you are constant voices of encouragement. You welcomed me into the Compass Christian Church family and actively planned in advance to support this project.

- <u>Sue Jorgenson,</u> anyone who knows me understands that commas are optional and apostrophes are plenty. Your love of grammar, and your editing and support were vital to making this book a great read.

- <u>Robert Budd</u>, you are a man of God. Your heart for the Lord rings out in your voice. I am so grateful for your persistent encouragement and support of Godfidence. The study guide reflects your guidance.

- <u>"Agent" Tollner</u>, you are an encourager. Thank you, Bruce, for constantly looking for ways to support my work and making the love of Christ known in the world.

- <u>Tom Koos</u>, our time together is always too brief. Your impact on my thinking and faith journey ever present.

- <u>Ron Bridges</u>, you've been a steadfast voice of faith. Thank you for your support and encouragement.

Chris Hodges

I met Chris after Godfidence was largely complete. Our paths crossed at a small meeting just a few short weeks before our launch date. Many people had joined me in praying for the person God wanted to write the foreword. Chris's kind southern accent is magnetic. But the depth of his conviction for the Gospel and his love for the Lord ignites your soul. I would have never known to reach out to Chris to write this foreword. The good thing is, I didn't have to—God wove us together.

With an Eye on the Finish Line

I'm constantly looking for examples of men and women who are pressing forward for the prize. By observation, those who stand out share something in common—they are sweet. I define sweet as being humble and possessing a servant's heart. Larry Stillman, Jerry Howells, John Heineman, Tom Phelps, Bill Harper, and Jimmy Blanchard, thank you for your examples.

APPENDIX

Connect with Jim

Websites
Godfidence.info
jimdakers.com
impactfulnotes.com

Other Books by Jim Akers
Tape Breakers
Maximize Your Impact with People You Love, Teams You Lead, and Causes the Stir Your Heart

2016 Book of the Year
Author Academy Elite Award Winner
#1 New Amazon Release

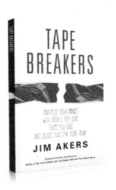

Covenant Eyes
Get 30 days of free access to Covenant Eyes
Go to www.CovenantEyes.com
and use promo code GODFIDENCE
(Promo Code good through website purchases only.)

ENDNOTES

Introduction

1. Lewis, C. S., "The Problem with Pain." (1940; reps., San Francisco: Harper, 2001), p 91.
2. Life Story, "Chuck Colson Life Story," Life Story Foundation, Accessed February 11, 2021, http://www.chuckcolsonstory.com.
3. Stacie Marshall, "7 Touching Testimonies by Christian Celebrities," God Updates, August 28, 2018, https://www.godupdates.com/christian-celebrities-testimonies-faith/.
4. Stephanie Nolasco, "'Duck Dynasty' star Phil Robertson explains how he found faith before fame: 'God speaks through his people," Fox News, March 28, 2019, https://www.foxnews.com/entertainment/duck-dynasty-star-phil-robertson-explains-how-he-found-faith-before-fame-god-speaks-through-his-people.
5. Stacie Marshall, Ibid.
6. Megan Bailey, "Actor Time Allen Reveals Heartbreaking Story That Led Hm to Jesus," Belief Net, Accessed February 11, 2021, https://www.beliefnet.com/columnists/idolchatter/2017/04/actor-tim-allen-reveals-heartbreaking-story-led-jesus.html.
7. Stacie Marshall, Ibid.
8. Lynette Nicholas, "EXCLUSIVE: Adrienne Camp On New Book 'In Unison,' Marriage & Faith," Moms, April 18, 2020, https://www.

9. Life Story, "Pete Maravich Story," Life Story Foundation, Accessed February 11, 2021, http://www.petemaravichstory.com.
10. Stacie Marshall, Ibid.
11. A. W. Tozer, "God's Pursuit of Man." (Chicago: Moody Publishers, 2015), xii.
12. Charles Colson, "The Good Life." (Grand Rapids: Zondervan, 2008), p. 92.

Part One—You Only Finish Once

13. Bob Buford, "Finishing Well." (Nashville: Thomas Nelson, 2006), xx.
14. Dictionary.com. Citation. Retrieved January 5, 2021 from https://www.dictionary.com/browse/those-who-cannot-remember-the-past-are-condemned-to-repeat-it
15. Howard Hendricks—unable to cite the specific source of this quote, but it if fully attributable to him.

Chapter 1— The Con of Self-Confidence

16. Barbara Markway, "Why Self-Confidence Is More Important Than You Think," Psychology Today, September 20, 2018, https://www.psychologytoday.com/us/blog/shyness-is-nice/201809/why-self-confidence-is-more-important-you-think.

Chapter 2—The Power of Godfidence

17. "What does the Bible say about confidence?" Got Questions, Retrieved May 10, 2020, https://www.gotquestions.org/Bible-confidence.html.
18. Steve Farrar, "Finishing Strong: Going the Distance for Your Family." (Sisters: Multnomah Publishers, 1995), 29.

Part Two—Getting Lost in Confidence

19. Wikipedia. 2021. "Willie Sutton." January 5, 2021. https://en.wikipedia.org/wiki/Willie_Sutton.
20. Jim Taylor, "Perception Is Not Reality," Psychology Today, August 5, 2019, https://www.psychologytoday.com/us/blog/the-power-prime/201908/perception-is-not-reality.

[21] John Kenneth Galbraith Quotes. BrainyQuote.com, BrainyMedia Inc, 2021. https://www.brainyquote.com/quotes/john_kenneth_galbraith_109909, accessed January 5, 2021.
[22] T. S. Eliot, *Murder in the Cathedral*, (New York: Harcourt Brace & Company, 1963), p. 41.
[23] Con. Merriam Webster.com. 2020. Web. April 26, 2020.
[24] C. S. Lewis, "Mere Christianity." (New York: MacMillian, 1942), p.28.

Chapter 3— The Myth of Self Reliance

[25] George A. Hodak, "Olympian Oral History, Louis S. Zamperini." Reasonable Theology. June 1988. Web. April 26, 2020. https://reasonabletheology.org/wp-content/uploads/An-Olympian's-Oral-History.pdf.
[26] Laura Hillenbrand, "Unbroken: A World War II Story of Survival, Resilience, and Redemption," Kindle Edition. (New York: Random House Publishing Group.), pp. 370-371.
[27] Ibid, 375.
[28] Ibid, 375.

Chapter 4—The Myth of Positive Thinking

[29] Mara Leighton, "The 31 Most Influential Books Ever Written About Business," Business Insider, December 18, 2019, https://www.businessinsider.com/influential-business-books.
[30] Brian Tracy Facebook page. Accessed January 2021. https://www.facebook.com/BrianTracyPage/photos/a.454285253459/10152118977328460/?type=1&theater.
[31] Wikipedia. "James Stockdale." January 1, 2021. https://en.wikipedia.org/wiki/James_Stockdale.
[32] J. D. Walt, "Christianity Is Not the Power of Positive Thinking," Seedbed, August 2, 2017, https://www.seedbed.com/christianity-is-not-the-power-of-positive-thinking/
[33] A. W. Tozer, *Dangers of a Shallow Faith: Awakening From Spiritual Lethargy* (Minnesota: Bethany House Publishers, 2012), 202.

Chapter 5—The Myth of Experience

[34] Marshall Goldsmith, "The Success Delusion," October 29, 2015, https://www.marshallgoldsmith.com/articles/the-success-delusion/.

Chapter 9—Timeless Means Timeless

35 "promise," Merriam-Webster.com. 2020. May 17, 2020.
36 Rick Warren, "Don't Fear! Remember God's Promises," RickWarren.com, December 19, 2019, https://pastorrick.com/dont-fear-remember-gods-promises/.
37 Rick Warren, "God's Promises About Your Future," July 16, 2019, video, 1:09:21, https://www.youtube.com/watch?v=DQ4G1oo_154.

Chapter 10—Bad Things Do Happen to Good People

38 Rick Warren, "Purpose Driven Life," (Grand Rapids, Zondervan Publishing, 2002), p. 42.
39 BPC, "Westminster Shorter Catechism Project," BPC.org, May 21, 2019, https://bpc.org/?page_id=263.

Chapter 11—Hey, You're Drifting

40 "Magruder Enters a Plea of Guilty," New York Times, August 17, 1973, https://www.nytimes.com/1973/08/17/archives/magruder-enters-a-plea-of-guilty-he-faces-5year-term-and-fine-in.html.
41 Jeb Stuart Magruder, "Famous Quotes By," Quotes.com, Retrieved, April 6, 2018, https://www.quotes.net/authors/Jeb+Stuart+Magruder.
42 C.S. Lewis, "The Screwtape Letters," (1942; rprt., New York: HarperCollins, 2001), 60–61.
43 "Billy Graham's daughter Ruth has been through the fire, says it's time for honesty," beliefnet.com, March 2012, https://www.beliefnet.com/columnists/news/2012/03/billy-grahams-daughter-ruth-has-been-through-the-fire-says-its-time-for-honesty
44 Ibid.

Chapter 12—Blurry Vision—Spiritual Blindness

45 Michelle Hamilton, "The Visionary: Henry Wanyoike," Runners World, January 12, 2015, https://www.runnersworld.com/runners-stories/a20843657/the-visionary-henry-wanyoike/
46 Proverbs 29:18, The Voice, [Emphasis mine].

Part Three—The Solution: Five Building Blocks for Building the Reliable Confidence You Need for Finishing Strong

47   Eric Blehm, "Fearless, The Undaunted Courage and Ultimate Sacrifice of Navy SEAL Team SIX Operator Adam Brown." (Colorado Springs: WaterBrook Press, 2012), p. 55.
48   Ibid, p. 75.
49   Ibid, p. 222.
50   Ibid, p. 230.
51   Ibid, p. 233.
52   Ibid, p. 233.

Chapter 13—The Process: Recalculating—Fix Your Eyes On Jesus

53   Recalculating. Merriam Webster.com. 2020. Web. May 5, 2020.
54   Recalculating. UrbanDictionary.com. 2020. Web. May 5, 2020.
55   Agnostic. Merriam Webster.com. 2020. Web. May 5, 2020.
56   Josh McDowell, Josh's Bio, JoshMcDowellMinistries.com, December 18, 2019, https://www.josh.org/about-us/joshs-bio/
57   Jerry Bridges, "Trusting God." (Colorado: Tyndale House Publishing, 2008), p. 134.
58   Ravi Zacharias. "Why I Believe in Jesus," April 4, 2019, video, 37:37, https://www.youtube.com/watch?v=M3kM6Rax1AU.
59   A. W. Tozer. "God's Search for Man," (Chicago: Moody Publishers, 2015), p. 27.
60   Psalm 91:1, ESV
61   Douglas Martin, "Randy Pausch, 47, Dies; His 'Last Lecture' Inspired Many to Live With Wonder." *The New York Times*, July 26, 2008.
62   Jeffrey Zaslow, "Professor Aimed 'Last Lecture' At His Children ... and Inspired Millions," Wall Street Journal, July 26, 2008, https://www.wsj.com/articles/SB121701813179885643.
63   ibid.

Chapter 14—The Invitation: What Do We Do With Jesus' Invitation?

64   Douglas Martin, "Randy Pausch, 47, Dies; His 'Last Lecture' Inspired Many to Live With Wonder," The New York Times, July 26, 2008.
65   Alistair Begg, "Be in Christ," Truth for Life, July 27, 2008, https://www.truthforlife.org/resources/sermon/be-christ/#[18]

66 William O'Flaherty, "Far Better Things," Essential C. S. Lewis, February 13, 2016, https://essentialcslewis.com/2016/02/13/ccslq-21-far-better-things/

Chapter 15—Uncovering Your Purpose: Our Identity in Christ—Purposeful and Powerful

67 David Brooks, "The Road to Character." (New York: Random House, 2015), p. xiii.
68 Ibid, p. xii.
69 Ibid, p xvi.
70 Rick Warren, "Purpose Driven Life," (Grand Rapids, Zondervan Publishing, 2002), p. 173.
71 "in Christ," Bible Gateway, Accessed July 17, 2020, https://www.biblegateway.com/quicksearch/?quicksearch=in+Christ&version=NIV.
72 Jerry Bridges, ibid, Location 224
73 1 Peter 5:11, NIV.

Chapter 16—Claiming God's Promises: A Promise is a Promise—Leaning on the Promise Maker

74 Barna Research, "A Snapshot of Faith Practice Across Age Groups," July 23, 2019, https://www.barna.com/research/faithview-on-faith-practice/
75 David Kinnaman and Gabe Lyons, "Good Faith." (Grand Rapids, Baker Publishing Group, 2016),
76 "Does Biblical Literacy Matter?" Seattle Pacific University: Response, Spring 2007, https://spu.edu/depts/uc/response/spring2k7/features/biblical-literacy-quotes-expanded1.asp
77 Dr. David R. Reagan, "Applying the Science of Probability to the Scriptures, Do statistics prove the Bible's supernatural origin," Lamb and Lion Ministries, https://christinprophecy.org/articles/applying-the-science-of-probability-to-the-scriptures/
78 Ibid.
79 Ibid.
80 Lee Strobel, "The Case for Faith." (Grand Rapids, MI: Zondervan, 2000), p. 262.
81 Alistair Begg, "Trusting God in the Dark," Truth for Life, January 20, 2019, https://www.truthforlife.org/resources/sermon/trusting-god-dark/

Chapter 17—Dress the Part: Putting on the Full Armor of God

82 Richard Stearns, "The Hole in the Gospel." (Nashville: Thomas Nelson Publishing, 2009), p. 2.
83 Ibid, p. 25.
84 C. S. Lewis, "The Problem with Pain." (New York: Harper Collins, 1996), p. 44.

Part Four—Introduction: Living in Daily Godfidence

85 J. M. Rodríguez García, "Knowledge is Power: Francis Bacon to Michel Foucault. *Neohelicon* 28," Springer Link, 109–121 (2001). https://doi.org/10.1023/A:1011901104984.
86 Alistair Begg,"The Source of Wisdom,"Truth for Life, May 13, 1984, MP3 audio, https://www.truthforlife.org/resources/sermon/source-of-wisdom-the/
87 A. W. Tozer, "God's Pursuit of Man." (Pennsylvania: Wing Spread Publishers), p. 10.
88 Ibid, p. 5.

Chapter 18—Truth, Faith, Prayer—Holy Anticipation and Expectation

89 Scott Hamilton, "Scott's Story," I Am Second, video, https://www.iamsecond.com/seconds/scott-hamilton/
90 Ibid.
91 Ibid.
92 Ibid.
93 Ibid.
94 Jerry Bridges, "Who Am I? Identity In Christ." (Hudson: Cruciform Press, 2012), Kindle Edition, Location 657.
95 Kevin Halloran, "The 40 Best E. M. Bounds Quotes on Prayer," Anchored in Christ, January 30, 2015, https://www.kevinhalloran.net/best-e-m-bounds-christian-quotes-on-prayer/
96 Ephesians 3:20, NCV
97 Psalm 46:10, NIV
98 Craig Hazen, "Thoughts on Prayer by Christian Leaders," Fearless Prayer, August 6, 2018, https://www.craighazen.com/2018/08/06/thoughts-on-prayer-by-christian-leaders/
99 Stormie Omartian, Inspiring Quotes, Accessed August 6, 2020, https://www.inspiringquotes.us/quotes/wjhk_EqOAG4Zt
100 Kevin Halloran, ibid.

101 Craig Hazen, "The Challenge to Pray Without Fear," Fearless Prayer, August 4, 2018, https://www.craighazen.com/2018/08/04/the-challenge-to-pray-without-fear/
102 Ibid.
103 Ibid.

Chapter 19—Take Every Thought Captive

104 Michael Gervais, "Interview with Retired U. S. Navy Captain, Jim Matteo," Finding Mastery, Podcast audio. April 17, 2018.https://findingmastery.net/jim-dimatteo/
105 Rodney J. Korba, "The Rate of Inner Speech." Sage Journals, December 1, 1990, https://journals.sagepub.com/doi/abs/10.2466/pms.1990.71.3.1043
106 Duke University, UCLA, and Princeton University Research (need to cite)
107 Rick Hanson, PhD., "Take in the Good," RickHansen.com, Accessed August 13, 2020, https://www.rickhanson.net/take-in-the-good/
108 Dr. Jack Haskins, "The Trouble with Bad News," Newspaper Research Journal, 1981;2(2):3-16.doi10.1177/073953298100200201.
109 Jory, MacKay, "Screen time stats 2019: Here's how much you use your phone during the workday," RescueTime.com, March 21, 2019, https://blog.rescuetime.com/screen-time-stats-2018/
110 Victora and Michale Robb, "The Common Sense Census:Media Use by Tweens and Teens," Rideout, 2019, https://www.commonsensemedia.org/sites/default/files/uploads/research/2019-census-8-to-18-full-report-updated.pdf.
111 Jory, MacKay, Ibid.
112 McCoy, Julia McCoy, New Outbrain Study Says Negative Headlines Do Better Than Positive, Business 2 Community, March 15, 2014, https://www.business2community.com/blogging/new-outbrain-study-says-negative-headlines-better-positive-0810707
113 Kristen Harold, "The State of Tech, How People Interact on Social Media in 2019, The Manifest, January 17, 2019, https://themanifest.com/social-media/how-people-interact-social-media
114 Lawrence Robinson and Melinda Smith, M.A., "Social Media and Mental Health, January 1, 2020, https://www.helpguide.org/articles/mental-health/social-media-and-mental-health.htm
115 David Kinnamann, "The Porn Phenomenon," SetFreeSummit.org, April 4, 2016, https://setfreesummit.org/monday/the-porn-phenomenon-david-kinnaman-roxanne-stone/

[116] Aleksandra. "A Year in Search: How many Google Searches per day?," January 10, 2019, https://seotribunal.com/blog/how-many-google-searches-per-day/

[117] Luke Gilkerson, "Your Brain on Porn," Covenant Eyes, July 18, 2014. https://www.covenanteyes.com/2014/07/18/your-brain-on-porn-revised/

[118] Kirsten Weir, "Is Pornography Addictive, apa.org, April 14, 2014, https://www.apa.org/monitor/2014/04/pornography

[119] David Kinnamann, ibid.

[120] Elaine Mingus, "Porn, the Pandemic That is Attacking Our Children," Covenant Eyes, April 6, 2020 https://www.covenanteyes.com/2020/04/06/porn-the-pandemic-that-is-attacking-our-children/

[121] C.S. Lewis, "Relying On God Has to Begin All Over Again," The Wisdom of C. S. Lewis, June 26, 2011, https://cslewiswisdom.blogspot.com/2011/06/relying-on-god-has-to-begin-all-over.html

[122] Mark Batterson, "The Circle Maker, (Grand Rapids, Zondervan Publishing, 2011),p. 16.

Chapter 20—Put First Things First

[123] Rachel Fulton Brown, "What's the point of reading 'Great Books'? The lesson of the Middle Ages," ABC Religion and Ethics, August 16, 2019, https://www.abc.net.au/religion/what's-the-point-of-reading-great-books-rachel-fulton-brown/11421202

[124] Ravi Zacharias, "The Key Answer," Just a Thought Podcast, August 17, 2017, https://www.rzim.org/listen/just-a-thought/the-key-answer

[125] Leonardo Blair, "I'm Probably an Atheist; I Don't Buy It, I Think the Only Reason for Religion is Death,' Says Broadcaster Larry King." Christian Post, February 23, 2105, https://www.christianpost.com/news/im-probably-an-atheist-i-dont-buy-it-i-think-the-only-reason-for-religion-is-death-says-broadcaster-larry-king.html

[126] James Montgomery Boice, "The Minor Prophets." (Grand Rapids, Baker Publishing, 2006), location 2:469.

Chapter 21—Build A Deepwater Faith

[127] David Kinnaman and Gabe Lyons, "Good Faith: Being Christian When Society Thinks You're Irrelevant and Extreme." (Grand Rapids, Baker Books, 2016), p. 49.

128. Ibid.
129. Casting Crowns, John Mark Hall. Lyrics to "Somewhere in the Middle," Essentials Music Publishing, Capitol Christian Music Group, 2007.
130. John Piper, "Is God Ever Surprised," desiring God, March 3, 2017, https://www.desiringgod.org/interviews/is-god-ever-surprised

Chapter 22—Keep Your Eye on the Finish Line

131. Richard J. Leyda, "Henrietta Corneilia Mears," Biola University, Talbot School of Theology. Accessed April 20, 2020. https://www.biola.edu/talbot/ce20/database/henrietta-cornelia-mears
132. Will Graham, "The Tree Stump Prayer: When Billy Graham Overcame Doubt," Bill Graham Evangelistic Association, July 9, 2014, https://billygraham.org/story/the-tree-stump-prayer-where-billy-graham-overcame-doubt/
133. Ibid.
134. Philippians 1:6, AMP

Part Five—Finishing Strong

135. "Understaning ALS," ALS Association, Accessed February 7, 2020, http://www.alsa.org/about-als/facts-you-should-know.html
136. Steve Gleason, "A Witness to Faith," Archdiocese of New Orleans, YouTube video, 48:52, https://www.youtube.com/watch?v=zTnngnaW1xk
137. Ibid.
138. Associated Press, "Steve Gleason Statue Unveiled," July 27, 2012, https://www.espn.com/nfl/story/_/id/8207214/new-orleans-saints-unveil-statue-steve-gleason-blocked-punt
139. James Crabree-Hannigan, "Drew Brees gives emotional speech as Steve Gleason receives Congressional Gold Medal, Sporing News, January 15, 2020, https://www.sportingnews.com/us/nfl/news/drew-brees-gives-emotional-speech-as-steve-gleason-receives-congressional-gold-medal/oa96u2tz8hz81njlgyr2klnpz
140. Team Gleason, "No White Flags, Accessed May 10, 2018, https://teamgleason.org
141. C-SPAN. "Drew Brees remarks at Steve Gleason Congressional Gold Medal Ceremony."January 15, 2020. Video, 5:19. https://www.youtube.com/watch?v=XhPzZd8pLsM

Chapter 24—One-On-One with Jesus

[142] Ephesians 6:10-18, ESV.
[143] Billy Graham, "Answers," Billy Graham Evangelical Society, July 27, 2005, https://billygraham.org/answer/does-god-know-when-every-person-is-going-to-die-or-is-it-all-left-up-to-chance/
[144] Alistair Begg, "Do You Believe…?"—Part One, From Series: A Light in the Darkness, August 13, 2006, https://www.truthforlife.org/resources/sermon/do-you-believe-part-1/#back-[20]
[145] Jerry Bridges, "Who Am I ?" Identity In Christ." (Hudson: Cruciform Press, 2012), Kindle Edition, Location 152.
[146] Alistair Begg, "Do You Believe…?"—Part One, From Series: A Light in the Darkness, August 13, 2006, https://www.truthforlife.org/resources/sermon/do-you-believe-part-1/#back-[20]
[147] Oswald Chambers, "My Utmost for His Highest." (Grand Rapids: Our Daily Bread Ministries, 1992.) January 13.

Made in United States
Orlando, FL
20 February 2023